BUILDING BIRDHOUSES
FOR
NORTH AMERICAN
BIRDS

by John Plewes

veritas° Tools

1080 Morrison Drive   12 East River Street
Ottawa   Ogdensburg
Ontario K2H 8K7   New York 13669

Distributed by: ᴜᴇRITꞨS⁕ Tools Inc.

1080 Morrison Drive	814 Proctor Avenue
Ottawa	Ogdensburg
Ontario K2H 8K7	New York 13669-2205

Canadian Cataloguing in Publication Data
Plewes, John
  Building birdhouses for North American birds

ISBN 0-921335-22-9

  1. Birdhouses - Canada - Design and construction.
2. Birdhouses - United States - Design and construction.
I. Title. II. Veritas Tools (Firm)

QL676.5.P43 1990   690.89   C90-090176-4

Printed in Canada
#50304

PUBLISHER'S NOTE

When this book was first contemplated several years ago, the impetus was the lack of soundly researched material on birdhouse construction. The various books on the market had conflicting, inaccurate information on such basic information as the hole sizes appropriate to specific species. In fact, the books emphasized structures that were attractive to people, not birds.

The best indication of this was the invariable inclusion of a perch directly beneath the entry hole. You will notice that none of the designs in this book include such a perch; the reason is that the traditional perch interferes with a bird's flight pattern — it is far better to use a few score lines on the box front for grip.

We are particularly grateful to the following people and organizations for reviewing text and providing valuable material:

Bruce Dilabio
Canadian Nature Federation

Pierre Mineau
Canadian Wildlife Service

This book is dedicated to our
native wild birds, and to all those
who assist them in their perilous
fight to avoid extinction.

ACKNOWLEDGEMENTS

My sincere thanks go to all who assisted in creating
the manuscript. I must thank my friend, Leonard Lee of
Lee Valley Tools, for initiating the project, which, it
appeared, was custom made for the talents of a 'bull-
headed Yorkshireman who got things done and didn't
muck about.' Attribute notwithstanding, I trust I do —
and I didn't — respectively.

Especially, I thank the hardworking staff of Lee Valley Tools for their helpful editing and excellent ideas
regarding the illustrations and layout of the book.

For converting my original pencilled scrawl into a
very workmanlike manuscript via countless hours of
excellent high-speed typing, I thank my wife, Jackie,
very much indeed.

For verifying my duck box dimensions and for kindly
taking the time to enhance my knowledge of them, I
thank Kathy Dixon of the Canadian Wildlife Service and
Leo Roos respectively.

For pertinent and up to date information on Barn Owls
and their nesting box dimensions, I am very grateful to
Dr. Carl D. Marti of Weber State College, Utah.

For improving my slender knowledge of bats and for
patiently answering my queries about them, I am in-
debted to Dr. D. A. Smith of Carleton University, and
thank him accordingly.

Drawings by the author
Illustrations by Lee Valley Tools
Photographs by Jacqueline Plewes,
except nos. 12, 13, 14, 19, & 20
Front Cover Photo by Graeme Scott

PREFACE

This book is intended as a practical guide to those who wish to promote the welfare of birds; it is hoped that implementing the ideas expressed herein will help towards restoring our native birds to their former numbers.

The reader is first given some idea of the problems facing the world's birds today (1990), as it is against this broad background that his, or her, efforts on their behalf will be made. After noting a few of the known characteristics of the birds concerned, instructions are given for making seven different sizes of nesting box, with variations, to suit more than twenty species. Each species has its own section, and its range and preferred habitat are given. Other topics include shelves for Swallows and Robins, growing some of your own birdseed, and, of course, an apartment house for Purple Martins.

Nesting boxes do not make the best roosting boxes, so these are the subject of a separate chapter. Feeders and birdbaths, and where to place them, are also dealt with.

Although bats are not birds, they certainly require our protection; these night shift workers help the human race about as much as birds do, so a bat house design is also included. A house like this will interest those who like to try something slightly unusual, beneficial, and very much needed.

Although this is a book for practical people who enjoy making things, chiefly in wood, additional pleasure is to be had from the knowledge that such efforts will help both birds and people. I believe that it is far more essential to teach our children how to hand feed a chickadee than it is to teach them how many bones are in its neck. Although the outlook for the world's wildlife today is so utterly dismal that to provide food and shelter for just a few species of birds appears to be a very tiny step, it is nevertheless a step in the right direction.

As a race, we surely owe birds, and indeed all the other creatures on our planet, more than we can ever pay for the appalling damage and destruction we have brought down on them and their habitat over past centuries. Statistics vary, but there is no doubt that whole species of animals, birds, reptiles and plants are becoming extinct at a steadily increasing rate. Man's pesticides and chemical wastes have poisoned virtually the whole earth; even the vast oceans are polluted, pole to pole, and their inhabitants are dying.

If our nesting boxes are to be used, we must make efforts to see that 'our' birds are not poisoned on their migrations, or in the far off countries in which they winter. The problem is international, and somehow we have to convince the powers-that-be that, if wildlife - and even mankind itself - is to survive, we must clean up our planet, live sanely, and respect its non-human inhabitants. Over-dependence on pesticides and herbicides along with the rapid rate of habitat destruction world-wide are issues we ignore at our peril.

I hope that the reader will enjoy making the various bird-aids depicted in this book, as well as the company of the birds thus attracted. And if a flood of letters to the appropriate authorities concerning the many threats to our bird populations can ensure the rightful occupancy of our nesting boxes for years to come, I shall feel amply rewarded. Contact your local wildlife service for information on names and addresses of local and national government agencies.

CONTENTS

SOURCES OF INFORMATION

A Field Guide to the Birds
    Roger Tory Peterson
    Houghton Mifflin Co.
    Boston 1956

A Guide to Field Identification of Birds
of North America
    C. S. Robbins, B. Bruun,
    H. S. Zim, A. Singer
    Golden Press, New York 1966

Country Journal Book of Birding
    A. Pistorius
    Norton
    New York 1981

Hand Taming Wild Birds at the Feeder
    A. G. Martin
    The Bond Wheelwright Co.
    Freeport, Maine 1968

I Live With Birds
    Roy Ivor
    Ryerson Press,
    Toronto 1968

Song Birds in Your Garden
    John K. Terres
    T. Y. Crowell
    New York 1963

Just Bats
    M. B. Fenton
    University of Toronto Press
    Toronto 1983

Birds of America
    E. H. Forbush, H. K. Job, W. L. Finley,
    L. N. Nichols, R. I. Brasher, R. B. Horsfall,
    H. Thurston and others
    Garden City Books
    Garden City, NY 1936

Field Guide to the Birds of North America
    National Geographic Society
    2nd Edition
    Washington, D.C. 1987

The Birds of Canada
    W. Earl Godfrey
    Canadian National Museum of Natural Sciences
    Ottawa, Ont. 1986

ILLUSTRATIONS

CHAPTER 1.
BIRDS AND THE WORLD THEY LIVE IN

Before sawing any wood to make any of the bird-aids described in this book, it is important to have some idea of how birds live and what part you will play in their lives after you have set up your nesting boxes. You will find that all is not peaceful in the avian world; it seems to be a scene of unending strife, and you will most likely have to take sides to assist desirable tenants against undesirable ones. This, of course, is a decision which you must make yourself.

Naturally, the human race considers things from its own point of view; we think in terms of how we are affected, or 'is it fair play?' In reality, it is often hard to separate avian villains from avian good guys. Examples are easy to find. Robins are fond of cutworms, June bug larvae and other insects which damage our lawns and grasses; they also eat a lot of our very essential earthworms. Crows undoubtedly rob the nests of beneficial birds now and again, but they also eat grasshoppers and many crop damaging insects in newly ploughed fields. The diet of the cowbird seems, in general, to benefit us, but this is far outweighed by the damage its parasitic lifestyle inflicts on other beneficial birds. Cowbirds lay their eggs in the nests of birds such as Yellow Warblers and Chipping Sparrows, where they hatch out ahead of the owner's eggs. The vigorous young cowbird then heaves out any other eggs or tiny young, and takes over the nest. When two cowbirds hatch out, each one entangles its claws very firmly in the bottom of the nest to prevent ejection by its equally irritable companion. Thus every cowbird raised has caused the death of about four warblers, or other very desirable birds. See "The Birds of Canada" by W. Earl Godfrey, P. 556 for a discussion of the habits of cowbirds. None of these three birds is likely to bother the occupants of your boxes, but there are others who will.

Most people will wish to make the smaller types of box with entrance holes of 1½″ or 1¾″ diameter. Unfortunately both of these sizes suit two very common pests. These are the House Sparrow and the European Starling, both of which were thoughtlessly imported into North America from Europe, the sparrow in about 1850 and the starling about 1890. These are two sorry dates for our native birds, for both imports are incredibly aggressive and persistent in driving off all competitors for food and nesting sites. Being ourselves responsible for this deplorable state of things, we can only do our best to correct matters in favour of the native species. To improve your chances, it is best not to put up your boxes until the birds you wish to attract return to your area from their migrations.

Although the House Sparrow and the European Starling are very numerous and undoubtedly constitute the worst problem faced by bird box people (birdboxers? Birdwatchers are known as 'birders', so perhaps we can call bird box builders 'birdboxers'), a native bird, the tiny House Wren, also causes a good deal of trouble, in my opinion. I have seen them peck holes in other birds' eggs and stuff all the cavities they can find, including nest boxes, with stout twigs. It is reasonable to conclude that they are very determined that no bird shall nest anywhere within, I would say, 600 feet of their own abode. There are other winged hazards to small birds and their young, but I rate their overall damage below that of the cowbird, House Sparrow, starling and wren quartet.

Cats and squirrels also mean trouble. Cats can sometimes manage to reach in and claw out the young birds, and squirrels are not averse to an egg or two. Tree Swallows are easy to protect from both of them for they like to nest out in the open, away from trees and shrubs; a metal pole to support the box is all that is required. Other birds, such as the chickadee, are harder to protect, because they prefer a secluded box with foliage around it, which makes predator access easier.

Further danger to nesting birds can come from parasitic blood-sucking insects, or a prolonged spell of wet, cold weather. Occasionally snakes get into the act by eating the eggs, but this is not very common in most areas.

Even when fully fledged and flying, birds may fall to small boys with BB guns or stun themselves on windows. Houses with patio doors are particularly hazardous for them; according to some naturalists they take a huge uncounted toll. Some pesticides also constitute a devastating threat to birds, indeed to all animal life, including the human race.

When migration begins, the dangers faced by birds are even greater. In addition to the natural hazards of fogs, fatigue over water and food shortages due to unseasonable weather conditions, sleet and storms, man has been lengthening the odds against the birds dramatically. The myriad obstacles we have built on migration routes (including hydro and telephone wires, busy highways and building developments) are responsible for the destruction of millions of birds, mirror-walled buildings and illuminated towers being among the worst offenders. Fortunately, public pressure has led to the use of strobe lights on some towers, mitigating the carnage somewhat where they are used. The deadly, disorienting glare of lighthouses takes a continuing toll, although with the introduction of automatic lighthouses, there is some controversy over whether fewer birds are now being killed by more modern beacons, or simply fewer deaths recorded because there is no one around to count them anymore. Public pressure is an essential ingredient in ensuring that migrating birds are taken into account when large-scale projects are built; it is vital that we educate ourselves and our public officials on the unnecessary dangers to wildlife that can be avoided by careful planning.

Because birds in general migrate, their protection must extend far beyond the confines of their breeding areas, such as your garden. Their conservation is decidedly an international matter. Whilst travelling, birds inevitably eat seeds and insects which have been poisoned to various degrees by chemical pesticides, according to the level of spraying in the area through which they must pass. Countries outside North America are often even less careful than we are in the application and dispersal of pesticides. Poisons thus ingested may be stored in the birds' bodies, killing them at a later date. Perhaps even more urgent threats to birds are the destruction of habitat through filling in marshes for agriculture or building, the razing of forests and wild areas, and the uncontrolled use of herbicides.

It is important to contact both local agencies and the embassies of countries involved in such practices. Well thought-out letters encouraging the banning or severe restriction of DDT (where it is still in use) and other particularly damaging compounds are one of the most effective means of bringing pressure to bear on any government to reconsider its policies on regulating pesticide use. Urging sound economic and environmental reasons for the preservation of wildlife habitats is similarly important. One authority on migratory birds suggests citing Costa Rica as an example of a country whose conservation programme has been and will probably continue to be economically rewarding. Writing letters to encourage legislation that protects migrating birds, such as the Canadian Migratory Bird Act does, might also be a fruitful avenue for those concerned about the threat to their numbers from hunting, either for sport or food, in countries where they are unprotected.

Do not consider this means of protest futile. Brian Davies, and his International Fund for Animal Welfare, stopped Canada's government-backed annual seal hunt, and they did it largely by means of organised letter writing. This means of protest is not generally considered a part of making bird boxes, but if you think about it, there is no point in making boxes for birds that died thousands of miles away, because they won't be back — ever.

The preceding information will have given the reader a general idea of some of the hazards facing birds in their everyday existence. There are undoubtedly other factors of which we know little. We do not know quite how they manage their marvellous navigational feats, for example. Birds, it seems, are able to return to the exact location of their nest site, even though the landscape has been changed and the pole moved. Such accuracy defies the usual stars-and-terrain ideas of navigation; something more is surely involved. But however we look at it, we are responsible for the effects of our decisions on wildlife generally. It is important both to educate ourselves on what those effects are and to act to mitigate them. Building birdhouses and feeders is one step that can help in itself and can lead to a greater awareness of the problems faced by birds generally.

CHAPTER 2
BIRDS AND YOUR NEST BOXES

Chapter 1 outlined the difficulties which birds in general have to face. We must now consider birds in particular, that is your tenants, and the practical aspects of playing host to them. When making nesting boxes, the most essential thing to bear in mind is that you are building to suit birds — not people, not even yourself. Obviously, you can't pick any bird you fancy from the list; it has to be regularly present in the region in which you live. Individual birds unquestionably have their own preferences, so we cannot necessarily expect immediately to attract, say, a bluebird, just because we set up a box made to what we presume are its preferred parameters. To start with, a bluebird may not pass by, or may examine the box and reject it. Then again, Tree Swallows or chickadees may take the box, for all three species will, I find, use the Tree Swallow box given later in this book. Similarly, a pair of Great Crested Flycatchers rented a room in our vacant Purple Martin house one year, and raised their four youngsters therein. Such pleasant surprises happen often, and are always instructive; they teach us that the box dimensions and its height and siting are not exactly carved in stone.

CONSTRUCTION

Bird boxes generally fall into two categories; decorative ones for people, and practical ones for birds. Before proceeding further, it is important to decide which type you are going to build. Some fancy store-bought nesting boxes remind me of fishing lures — dazzle painted so as to catch people (fishermen) rather than fish. If you decide on embellishments, you inevitably reduce your chances of renting your box, particularly if the basic dimensions have to be changed to accommodate the trimmings. Your additions, however, should never include setting a perch or dowel below the entrance hole. Such a post impedes the bird's access to the hole and so wastes valuable time when the adults are working flat out to feed their young. Observation will verify this; note that the birds always swoop up to the entrance hole, so a perch would be in their way. Bark slabs, shown in the drawings as alternative fronts, lend a pleasant appearance to nest boxes, without making them obtrusive.

They do not, however, seem to attract birds any better than plain-front boxes, and possibly not quite as well.

In general, stains are preferable to paint for boxes. Maintenance is easier and there is no danger of the young being poisoned by peeling flakes of lead-based paint. A Purple Martin house may be the only exception, as explained later, latex being the paint then used.

The best woods to use for durability are probably redwood and cedar. Redwood is excellent, but is somewhat expensive and not always easy to obtain. Used cedar siding is fine for box sides and its recessed edges make for draft proofing. Cheaper boxes, neatly made of new or used ¾" thick pine offcuts, and left to weather, look fine and score well with the birds. Do not use creosote, as it leaches out and remains toxic for a long time. Avoid pressure-treated wood for bird boxes and feeders and never use stain on the interior. Even untreated, pine boxes last many years. Your tenants, remember, do not want to attract attention to their nest box, therefore fancy paint jobs are out, and low key, subdued colours are in, so that the box merges in with its surroundings and background. This policy seems best when predators come in so many shapes and sizes, including other birds, small boys, mammals and reptiles and it is hardly wise to assume that all of them are totally colourblind. In the open, where heat can be a problem, the Ontario Ministry of Fish & Wildlife recommends painting bluebird boxes white, to keep the boxes cooler. White boxes are not found naturally however, and are undoubtedly more conspicuous. I therefore consider naturally weathered wood to be best.

There is, of course, no requirement at all to use precious mahogany, oak or walnut, though such woods undoubtedly make up into a very handsome box indeed. In fact, someone near and dear to you would be likely to point out that such a box was far too nice to hang outside in the sun and rain for the birds to mess up, and it could quite easily wind up as part of the living room decor.

Easy access for inspection and cleaning is a must. Simple catches or springs, as explained in Chapter 4, are fine but wood screws are usually too much trouble. Easy mounting and removing are also required; I find that a single nail and keyhole form the best arrangement for most boxes of reasonable size.

Most people advocate the use of ventilation holes but aside from the drainage-cum-ventilation holes in the floor, these should never be below the level of the entrance hole, because of drafts. I consider draft proofing to be more important than ventilation in Canada, particularly when the young are tiny. A $\frac{5}{16}''$ diameter hole in each corner of the box bottom is sometimes used to admit air as the hot air inside the box rises. The same effect can be achieved by chamfering the corners of the bottom, say $\frac{3}{8}'' \times \frac{3}{8}''$ before assembly. The principal use of either holes or chamfering, however, is to prevent flooding.

A few $\frac{1}{4}''$ or $\frac{3}{8}''$ diameter ventilation holes in the sides, just below the roof of the box, are not a bad idea. Remember though that the entrance hole area is already appreciably larger than that of the four bottom holes combined. We must also remember that avian bodies run at a higher temperature (about 106°F) than our own. Nevertheless in the warmer areas of North America, such ventilation could well be a good thing. I believe that more young birds die in Canada from cold and damp than die from heat.

SITING

The siting of a nesting box is quite important. We don't know why birds sometimes refuse to nest in what we think is an ideal location. Shifting a Martin House pole as little as 20 feet has been known to bring about a successful occupancy after years of failure at a former site which was seemingly just as suitable. Perhaps it involves the mysterious 'earth fields' which birds may use in their amazing navigational feats. Here is one example of such a feat; there are many others:

It seems that a Nova Scotia resident attempted to move his Purple Martin colony about 100 miles. The whole martin house was closed up, after dark, with the birds inside, and transported overnight. When the birds were released the next morning, they seemed a little confused but they soon had it all figured out. By lunch time they were all back at the ranch. Naturally, their apartment house had to go back too, and soon all was well again. It would appear a real estate deal includes your Purple Martins.

In positioning your boxes, it should be noted that nesting birds appropriate territories around their nests from which they drive all others of their own species. This ensures their food supplies. The size of these claimed areas varies with the size and power of the owners. A pair of hawks, for example, may rule over a square mile or so, which would encompass the many smaller domains claimed by much less powerful birds. Normally, almost any bird is quite willing to share its territory with a bird of a different species, provided that there is no competition for food. Almost always, several non-competitive species will share a large common area. As an example, pairs of Cedar Waxwings, Orioles and American Robins will amicably share the same area because their diets differ and they do not compete for available food. Even a relatively small garden can host, say, shelf nesting Robins & Phoebes on opposite sides of the same tool shed, whilst Chipping Sparrows nest in the bushes below.

Colony nesters such as Purple Martins have no individual territories — the more the merrier for them. Bank, Barn and Cliff Swallows are also colony minded; Tree Swallows, however, prefer a little more room, say 100 feet between nests. They will, of course, combine forces to repel Purple Martins from their own shared area, because both species eat similar food, that is, mosquitoes and other insects caught in flight.

Almost all birds are more territorial than the swallow tribe. Boxes intended for other species, and of a similar size and entrance hole, should not be placed within, say, 250 feet of each other, and certainly not within sight of each other, except as explained below.

Because of the increased use of steel fence posts in the countryside, the old hollow wooden posts are quite rare, and consequently, so are the bluebirds which used to nest in them. Farmers will almost always give permission for you to set up bluebird boxes on their fences, and nesting box trails many miles long have thus been set up along country roads by thoughtful individuals. Several such people, servicing their own boxes, can link territories to provide almost unlimited coverage; lines up to several hundred miles long have been known to exist.

If, on a bluebird trail, one box is placed about 1000 feet from the next one, many of them will be occupied by the more numerous Tree Swallows. They are also excellent birds to have around, and so should not be evicted, but bluebirds are what we really want. A good idea, therefore, is to try setting up boxes placed only 15 feet or 20 feet apart, in pairs each 1000 feet or so. Even Tree Swallows won't want to nest this close together, but one pair of each species would, especially if one of the boxes is placed a few feet higher than the other. Although this method uses twice as many boxes, it may well result in a marked increase in both species. Incidentally, Tree Swallows and other swallows have markedly declined in the Ottawa Valley of Ontario in the few years preceding 1990.

INSTALLATION

Predator-proofing a box is best accomplished by using a metal pole and keeping it far enough away from trees or structures so that squirrels and cats cannot jump aboard. A convenient system I have used for many years starts with a 24″×2″×2″ wood stake, sharpened at one end and rounded for some 9 inches at the other. This is treated with wood preservative and driven about 12 inches into the ground. A five or six foot length of eavestrough downpipe is then dropped over the stake and a similar stake (24″×2″×2″) with its top end left square, is fitted into the top of the pipe. This top piece carries a stout common nail, sloping slightly upwards, which fits into a keyhole in the back of the box. A fairly straight tree branch (roughly 24″ long × ⅝″ diameter) is nailed across its top piece to form a much appreciated perch. The whole assembly is shown in Photo 1. If the older style 2 inch downpipe is not available, the more modern larger size may be used, along with correspondingly larger wooden sections. This system makes it very easy to lift off the box and its pole assembly for winter storage. Relocation is easy, too; you just shift the stake.

Another good method of supporting a box is to use a steel T-bar fence post, see photo 2. A seven foot bar driven down 20 inches is fine. Fasten a 30 inch length of 2″×2″ wood to the flat side of the top of the T-bar with two pieces of fence wire or coathanger wire.

Notch the rear-most corners of the wood, (see photo. 3), to prevent the wires slipping as the wood shrinks, and run the wires through the holes in the T-bar at the front.

Photo 1

Photo 2

Photo 3

The wood carries a nail and perch, as previously described. The box is lifted off for the winter storage, which greatly prolongs its life.

A WORD OF CAUTION

Sometimes a box is left untenanted (you think) for some time and sooner or later inspection time rolls around. It is as well not to just reach up and unhook the box, stick your finger in the hole, and walk off with it, because you might have rented out the box unknowingly. Some people like to keep records of how many young birds are raised, but even the most ardent statistician will drop the box and take off right smartly rather than count how many wasps he has in his box. Incidentally, I find that predominantly black wasps are more peaceable than the predominantly yellow variety, who are very hard citizens to mess with.

If you have to get wasps out of a box, your foremost concern is containment — to stop them from getting airborne in your vicinity. A winter coat and a bee veil constitute worthwhile insurance, however, should your 'foolproof' theoretical plan misfire.

It is best to approach quietly on a cool morning or evening when the wasps are inside but relatively inactive, and quickly plug the entrance hole with a rolled up cloth. It may also be necessary to seal the odd ventilation hole with a wood sliver or masking tape, etc. A pyrethrin based insecticide spray bomb can then be used to deal with the inhabitants. Make sure that the bomb you buy comes equipped with a plastic extension tube; these tubes are less than $1/10''$ in diameter and fit into the spray nozzle. Insert the free end of the tube into the box at the side of the cloth roll and press the button. After an hour or so, the box can be cautiously examined and its late and unlamented occupants removed, together with their nest. Note that all insecticides must be used with care and all the instructions on the spray bomb should be scrupulously followed.

The same procedure works for a martin house too, but if there are inter-connecting ventilation holes, it is as well to file a rapid flight path in your mind before commencing operations. Also, bear in mind that the wasps might have stationed a squadron or two in the next apartment.

To alleviate insect and nettle stings, and in particular, poison ivy, I usually apply crushed jewelweed, which is also called Spotted Touch-me-not and in latin — Impatiens capensis. Aloe Vera may also help.

Sometimes a peaceable tree frog may use an empty box for bed and breakfast; being much more of a gentleman, he should be removed gently and allowed to proceed about his business.

INSPECTIONS and PARASITES

Too many inspections disturb the birds and could cause desertions. Personally, I look in to see that the eggs are okay and generally leave things alone thereafter, unless I suspect trouble. Remember that you are out to raise birds, not to collect statistics. Although I have seen pictures of people holding young birds in their hands, I strongly advise against any contact whatsoever, because the adults may refuse to feed youngsters who have been handled, and they then die quite quickly. Birds may be thought to have no sense of smell, but they know a handled youngster from an unhandled one, as I once found out to my sorrow. If you have to shift a fresh-from-the-box youngster because it is in danger, do by gently coaxing it onto a small stick; avoid all hand or finger contact with the bird itself.

The swallow tribe seems to be particularly prone to parasitism and an inspection of all boxes a few days after hatching is advisable.

EDITOR'S NOTE

According to the Nature Society News (the publication for the Nature Society, an organization of Purple Martin enthusiasts) and J. L. Wade, one of America's foremost martin authorities, the most effective alternative to chemical parasite controls (and least harmful to the environment or the birds themselves) has been shown to be diatomaceous earth. It kills insects mechanically, that is, by puncturing their outer shells with its microscopically small sharp edges. The insects become desiccated and die. Mammals and birds, however, can eat the stuff with no adverse effects. (Do not breathe the dust when applying it, however, use a mask.) It will not break down over time and retains its effectiveness indefinitely.

The recommendations for using diatomaceous earth include a pre-season treatment of two to three tablespoons sprinkled under the subfloors of the martin house before nesting has begun. A mid-season treatment of two tablespoons sprinkled on top of the nest can also be made once the young have hatched. The mid-season treatment is optional, but recommended if you have a martin house you can get to easily.

Diatomaceous earth is available from William Dam Seeds, Box 8400, Dundas, Ontario L9H 6M1. Their catalogue is free. For further information on biological pest management generally contact the Canadian Wildlife Service or Agriculture Canada. The "IPM Practitioner" is published monthly by the Bio-Integral Resource Center, Box 7414, Berkeley, California 94707. The address of The Nature Society is Griggsville, IL, USA 62340.

Parasites are not to be dismissed lightly; when present in numbers, they can, and do, kill young birds by sucking their blood. In any case, a day or two after the young are off and flying, the box should be taken down and cleaned out.

The amount of excrement and infestation left in a nesting box varies with the species. Bluebirds and chickadees, for example, leave a relatively clean and tidy nest when they leave, but Tree Swallows and Purple Martins leave a much worse mess to clean up.

CAUTION

Never empty the box contents on the ground; you will simply be promoting parasite production. Always take the box, or for convenience, several of them, straight to your fire site and empty them out — downwind from yourself. Burn the contents immediately. A 2″ or 2½″ putty knife is excellent for cleaning out boxes and scraping the inside clean. The nest debris, sometimes including a few sad little corpses and infertile eggs, is usually dry and burns well; again — make sure that no one is downwind to breathe the smoke. Before storing, I usually set the box down for a few days near an ant nest; they take care of the mites for me and the sunshine helps too.

Mites are not easy to see, but can be felt as a mild tickling sensation on your hand or arm. Scratching does not kill these tiny creatures, so an immediate soap and hot water session is a good precaution to prevent them getting into your clothes. A drop or two of antiseptic disinfectant in the water also helps. Fortunately, I do not find mites to be a frequent or serious problem. It is as well to put up a clean box, of the same type and in the same place as the one you cleaned, for a few weeks, for the birds to visit.

When fall rolls round again and the empty boxes are ready for winter storage, they should first be examined and repaired where necessary.

Most of the boxes shown in later pages hang on a single nail through their rear keyholes. For winter storage, therefore, all that is required is a row of common nails, 8 or 10 inches apart along the top of a wall inside a barn, garage or shed, (photo 4, pg. 57). Many nesting boxes, being small, can be conveniently set in place or removed with an inverted pitch fork, a tine on each side steadies the box whilst the centre one goes into the entrance hole and contacts the roof to provide lift.

Nesting boxes unfortunately don't make the best

winter roosting boxes as there are no perches in a nesting box for a group of birds to use and the entrance hole, being close to the top, dissipates the small supply of communal warmth. Even so, it is as well to leave the odd one out in a sheltered site, if only to see if roosting occurs and by whom.

PREDATORS and UNDESIRABLES

It usually takes a season or two for you, a new 'bird-boxer', (the word seems good enough to retain) to realise that House Sparrows and starlings, when present, really will drive out native birds and usurp the boxes you set up for them. Once the true situation is accepted, well — join the club — and all the other long-time birdboxers who have wrestled with the problem for years.

In a city environment both species are sometimes so abundant that it is useless to set up boxes at all. The suburbs stand a better chance, however, and then the fight is on — and a fight means casualties. We imported these two troublesome types and we must help to control them.

Over the years people have thought of many ingenious ways to repel these two tenacious species; some methods work, some don't. It is useless to catch them and release them miles away; they'll be back before you are — filling your boxes. Some have tried clipping one or both wing feathers, which presumably keeps them at bay for a season. Some use air rifles, or even .22's in the outskirts or open country, but this can be dangerous to other forms of life, particularly people. Naturally, the tiny .22 birdshot is safer than a solid bullet.

Trapping the pests using pigeon cote drop-wires inside a box has been tried, as have deep boxes with lightly balanced trap door bottoms. In the Purple Martin box section, I describe one owner's problems and some of his pest control statistics.

Even high voltage has been tried, using an ignition coil and a couple of contacts on the lower rim of the entrance holes; wrens were intrigued, and being small and lightweight they were 'tickled' as you might say. Still, they looked on it as an occupational hazard and they'd dance on and off it all day, in fact just as long as you cared to press the switch for them. Sparrows were not too keen on it and came back later. Starlings, being heavier, got a little more stimulation; they swore and took off sharpish, in their customary no-nonsense manner.

It is useful to exploit a characteristic or habit of a pest to control it. A characteristic of the wren, which I consider a pest, for example, is that it is small enough to pass through a 1" diameter hole, a fact which can be used to separate it from other birds. I know of no weakness in the House Sparrow, which fortunately is not seen much around my boxes. It is possible, however, to trap the female in the box after dark. Starlings, on the other hand, happen to prefer dark nesting places, and so will, I find, often avoid boxes painted white inside or lined with aluminum foil. This starling trait can therefore be used to help Purple Martin box owners to repel them. But a box for a Great Crested Flycatcher or flicker is not easy to defend against sparrows and starlings, and summers spent repeatedly throwing out their nests are all too common — and unprofitable. Relocating the box each time helps only rarely. In practice, the desirable birds simply leave areas of high sparrow and starling concentration and look further afield. The trouble is that further afield is getting harder and harder for them to find.

Trap boxes with drop wires or false floors will not hurt the bird entrant, so a 'good guy' can easily be released. The pests simply have to be dealt with, one way or another, and people use various methods. Some simply wring their necks, others use chemicals or engine exhaust fumes in plastic bags. Whatever way is used, it must be quick and painless, with no suffering involved. It is a pity, but if we do not try thus to correct our original importation mistakes of years ago, we do not deserve to enjoy our native species; if we do nothing they will eventually be wiped out and so denied to us.

Cowbirds are a sore trouble to birds who build their own nests in thickets, and wrens often ruin both these nests and those of the cavity nesters. The activities of both birds seem 'unfair' to our way of thinking, but we did not introduce them and avian society has presumably learned to cope with their hoodlum habits.

Squirrels seem to fall into the same category as cowbirds and wrens — an affliction to put up with. Short of shooting them, it is very hard to discourage them. The same might be said of cats. As dismantling someone's pet feline is definitely frowned upon, however, it is better to have a word with the owner with regard to installing a collar and bell on the said cat and restricting its free time somewhat. These measures should at least reduce its lethal effect on your birds.

The reader should now have some idea of what bird-boxing is all about. Subsequent sections of the book deal with the actual construction work involved. Table 1 lists 22 cavity nesters and gives the dimensions of their nesting boxes.

All measurements are in inches except where otherwise indicated.

FIG.	BIRD NO.	BIRD	FLOOR	FRONT HEIGHT	HOLE HEIGHT	HOLE DIA.	HEIGHT UP(FEET)
2	1	House Wren	4×4	9½	6	1	5 to 7
2	2	Bewick's Wren	4×4	8	6	1¼	5 to 7
2	3	Carolina Wren	4×4	8	6	1½	5 to 7
2	4	Tufted Titmouse	4×4	8	6	1¼	5 to 7
2	5	Carolina Chickadee	4×4	8	6	1¼	5 to 7
2	6	Black Capped Chickadee	4×4	8	6	1¼	5 to 7
2	7	Red Breasted Nuthatch	4×4	8	6	1¼	8 to 15
3	8	White Breasted Nuthatch	4½×4½	9	7	1½	8 to 15
3	9	Downy Woodpecker	4½×4½	9	7	1½	8 to 15
4	10	Tree Swallow	5×5	8	6	1½	6 to 10
4	11	Bluebird	5×5	9	7	1½	5 to 10
5	12	Great Crested Flycatcher	6×6	10	7	2	8 to 20
5	13	Hairy Woodpecker	6×6	14	11	2¼	15 to 20
5	14	Red-Headed Woodpecker	6×6	14	11	2¼	15 to 20
5	15	Red-Bellied Woodpecker	6×6	14	11	2¼	15 to 20
5	16	Northern Saw-Whet Owl	6×6	14	11	2½	10 to 20
6	17	Northern Flicker	8×8	16	12	3	5 to 20
6	18	American Kestrel	8×8	16	12	3	15 to 25
6	19	Screech Owl	8×8	16	12	3	10 to 25
12	20	Wood Duck	10×10	19(apx.)	15	4×3	to 5 (water) to 20 (land)
13	21	Barn Owl	15×20	16	5	6	5 and up
14	22	Purple Martin	6×6	6	2½	2¼	7 to 20

CHAPTER 3
NEST BOX CONSTRUCTION

Before choosing a particular box design, it is important to consider how each configuration will be affected by the weather, heat and cold — in brief, how effective will it be? A prolonged wet spell can bring death to young nestlings, so rain must be kept out as much as possible. Fig. 1 compares the angles at which rain can enter the entrance hole on a windy day; vertically falling rain must, of course, soak the whole box before the nest itself is affected by flooding.

Aside from the inverted 'V' type, the two most usual sloping roof options are those of Fig. 1 (a) and (b). The latter gives better rain protection, but the shaded area constitutes a waste of space and wood, and adds unwanted bulk and weight.

In Fig. 1 (c), the top strip which holds the front in place (see Figs. 4 and 5), has been extended to coincide with the front edge of the roof, thus providing still better protection. Note that thickening the front (Fig. 1 (d)) to lengthen the hole would not improve it rainwise, though it might well give better predator protection. The problem of prolonged rain undoubtedly suggests the advisability of using a waterproof stain; this is okay only as long as it is done in the fall to allow all toxicity to disperse long before spring installation.

As mentioned previously, a well thought-out nesting box must be reasonably predator proof, attractive to birds, easy to set up, inspect, clean out, repair and store. A design which fulfils these requirements often does not lend itself to much change without a significant deterioration in one or more of the requisite parameters.

I have retained some form of removable front, for example, in all the box designs. This is because it allows better access for checking on parasites, cleaning out and, say, sprinkling diatomaceous earth, than would be the case if the roof lifted off. Likewise, I have not shown any hollowed-out log types, because I find that they warp and so let in drafts and are not easy to clean out or repair. It is important that the reader should know the reason for any given feature, so that it is not arbitrarily discarded as being superfluous.

The dimensional tolerances used in making bird

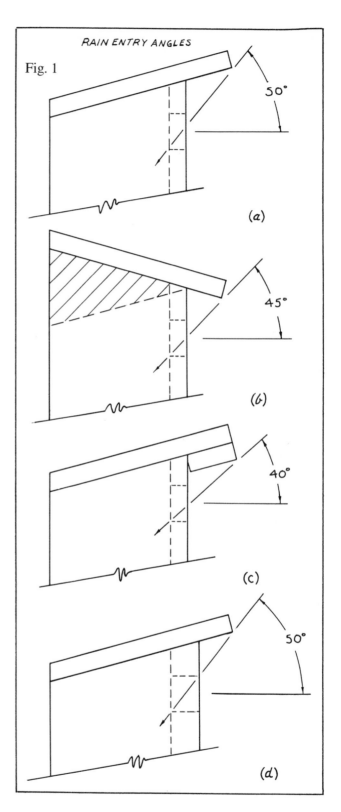

RAIN ENTRY ANGLES

Fig. 1

(a) 50°

(b) 45°

(c) 40°

(d) 50°

boxes are not at all stringent, but I recommend that you carry out each step in turn, accurately and well, before proceeding to the next one. Bear in mind, however, that small size changes occur in wood as it ages, dries or weathers. Do not, for example, try for too close a fit for the door, where applicable, as the wood will swell initially, due to stain or moisture, which may cause it to jam. In such cases, plane off the absolute minimum of wood to free it, because over the years, the door will slowly shrink, and the gap will widen somewhat.

As long as the main parameters, such as hole size, are incorporated, details such as door holding and mounting fixtures can be changed to suit individual preferences.

Each of the box designs has its own text on how it can be made. Although some repetition is inevitable with this method, it avoids confusion and is self-contained and concise. Wood grain orientation, where shown, should be observed; the grain is assumed to be lengthwise on long pieces such as sides and fronts.

For quick reference, a few pests or problems may be mentioned as possibly affecting the bird species under consideration. As parasites and flies can affect virtually all nestlings, they are not mentioned again in every case.

The term 'bird-aids' can be defined as any device which helps birds, and although the various bird-aids detailed in this book differ in purpose and dimension, there are a few guidelines which apply to them all.

Waterproof glue, or preferably 5 minute epoxy resin, and glueblocks may be called for in certain instances; ringed or spiral steel nails are all that is required in almost every other application. Some box makers use copper or aluminum nails, but I find that both these types tend to loosen and pull out ahead of steel nails, which will last many years before rusting out. A few brass screws are called for occasionally, such as in the Purple Martin house, to facilitate its yearly assembly and disassembly, otherwise such screws are seldom required.

When hanging keyhole-mounting boxes, drive the nail slightly downwards, so that the head is higher than the point. Make sure that the nail head is virtually flush with the inside surface of the back when the box is hung. A projecting nail could cause injury to the birds.

Figs. 2 to 6, 7 and 14 share several common concepts, but they depict variations in ventilation and different fronts and fastening methods from one box to another. It should be understood that these various features are not specific to the box in which they appear, but can be used in any suitable combination in other boxes. The bark slab front of Fig. 5, for example, and the ventilation holes of Fig. 4 may be incorporated into the box shown in Fig. 2. By spreading such features over separate drawings, confusion can be avoided.

Figs. 15 to 25 in Chapter 4 supplement Figs. 2 to 6 in that they give various fastening details and other data which would be difficult to show in a single drawing. Unless otherwise specified, ¾″ dressed lumber, such as pine, is called for when making all the bird-aids which follow, and all dimensions are in inches. Nesting boxes are given in the order of their size, the smallest being dealt with first. Most nesting boxes will serve several species, usually with small changes in height or hole size; hence a separate drawing for each bird would be unduly repetitious. The abbreviations used in the drawings are almost self explanatory: BH = back height, FH = front height, HD = hole diameter and HH = hole height. The species are numbered (1) (2) etc. for convenient reference. Typical finished boxes are shown in photos nos. 5 to 7 on pages 57 & 58. Purple martin houses are shown in photos 8 to 14 on pages 59 to 61.

It is important to realize that, like people, individual birds have their own preferences, and so may use any box they fancy, quite often one we designed to suit a different species. The bird's choice is also influenced by the siting of the box, and its height above ground.

The nest sites mentioned are those in the bird's preferred environment, and may not always be attainable. If suitable habitat is lacking around your home, permission can often be obtained to set up boxes in privately owned woodlots, brush or on a farmer's fence. The shaded areas in the following maps indicate each bird's approximate year round occupational and/or breeding areas. The boundaries of these areas may vary from time to time and are not in any way to be considered as being definitive.

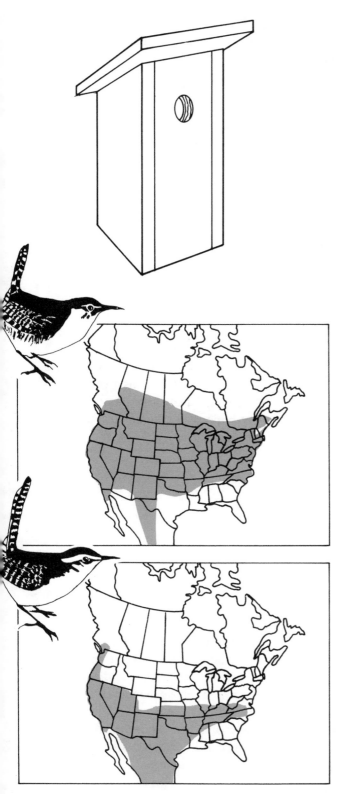

SECTION 1

The box shown in Fig. 2 is attractive to at least seven species, as long as their preferred hole size, siting and above-ground height requirements are met.

(1) HOUSE WREN

NEST SITE: A House Wren will nest just about anywhere; in the pocket of an old coat, a rusty can, a natural cavity, or a nesting box. Five to seven feet above ground seems to be the preferred height, the nest being close to shrubbery, a cedar hedge or other protective cover. Wrens seldom venture far from cover; they avoid open areas.

House Wrens do not have to compete with other species for a nesting box, as their 1″ diameter hole excludes all other cavity nesters and makes predation more difficult. The nest box is usually crammed with coarse twigs, a less dense assembly than other birds usually build, and one which makes for somewhat less underside infestation.

(2) BEWICK'S WREN

Some books quote a HD of 1⅛″, but a 1¼″ dia. hole allows the chance of hosting birds (4), (5), (6) and (7) also, where available, and so makes for a much more useful box.
NEST SITE: Natural cavities or nesting boxes, often in the vicinity of buildings, also in dense brush.

(3) CAROLINA WREN

Bewick's Wren is slightly larger than the House Wren and the Carolina Wren is larger still, about sparrow size. All three birds continually investigate their surroundings perpetual-motion fashion, in their endless search for insects and larvae which are mostly harmful to mankind's interests.

NEST SITE: Natural cavities or nesting boxes often in the vicinity of buildings, also in damp thickets and dense undergrowth.

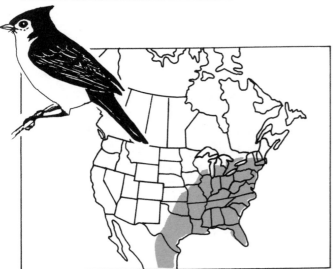

(4) TUFTED TITMOUSE

An associate of chickadees, this active small character has a liking for streamside deciduous greenery.

NEST SITE: Some 5 to 7 feet up in a partially concealed natural cavity or birdbox just within bush that can provide cover in emergencies.

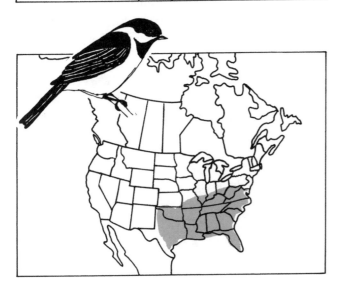

(5) CAROLINA CHICKADEE

This smaller version of the Blacked Capped Chickadee likes to live and nest in pine bush and swamps in the same general area of his above mentioned associate but not quite as far north.

NEST SITE: In a natural cavity or birdbox 5-7 feet up in a partially concealed location with bush nearby to provide emergency protection.

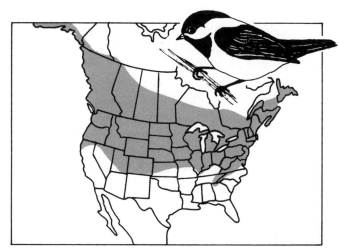

(6) BLACK CAPPED CHICKADEE

Probably the best known native bird in North America, this small, feathered acrobat can be hand-fed by those who like them enough to persevere a while offering their favourite sunflower seeds. Chickadees cover their eggs with moss when temporarily away on a feeding trip, and the nest may appear empty. It is important not to throw such moss away under the mistaken impression that the box is empty.

NEST SITE: Usually 5 to 7 feet up in a partly concealed natural cavity or birdbox near or in evergreen bush such as cedar or pine.

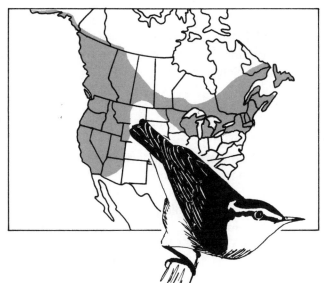

(7) RED BREASTED NUTHATCH

Another small acrobat, equally at home moving up, around or down a tree trunk. Prefers coniferous evergreen bush. May apply a sticky tree exudation around the entrance hole to its nest cavity.

NEST SITE: In evergreen bush, such as fir and pine, from eight to fifteen feet above ground. The box floor should have an inch or two of shavings, pine needles or similar material to encourage habitation.

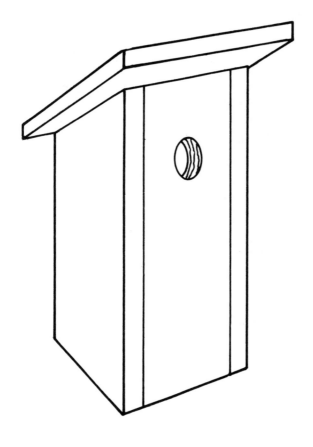

CONSTRUCTION

To make the box, cut out the pieces accurately, include ventilation measures and a roof rain slot (see Figs. 4 and 5) and sand them smooth as necessary. The keyhole consists of $\frac{3}{16}''$ and $\frac{7}{16}''$ merged holes and is placed centrally some $1\frac{1}{2}''$ from the top of the back. The entrance hole should not be drilled just now, but an exit ladder for the young should be incorporated on the inside of the front, along the lines shown in Fig. 8.

Fasten the floor squarely to the back, using two $1\frac{1}{2}''$ or $1\frac{3}{4}''$ common nails. These nails, and all other nails, should have their positions marked out reasonably accurately in order to avoid the wood splits which result from careless nailing.

Using an adjustable square, mark out accurately, and carefully drill the two nail holes 'N'. These are clearance holes for two $2''$ finishing nails; a $\frac{3}{32}''$ or no. 39 drill is typical. Unless these holes are lined up and carefully drilled, the front will bind instead of swivelling down easily as intended. Nail the sides to the back first, lining up their rear and top edges. Use two nails on each side on a line $\frac{3}{8}''$ from the rear edge, at, say, $1''$ and $5''$ from the bottom; this will avoid conflict with other nails.

Six more $2''$ nails are now used to fit the roof on, two in each side and the back. Use spiral or ringed nails here, as they grip better into end-grain wood. Take care to position the top correctly, by measurement, and ensure that the sides are parallel before driving the nails home.

Fit the strip 'S', which measures some $\frac{3}{8}''\times\frac{1}{2}''\times4''$, (roof detail, Fig. 2) to the roof, using glue and two small $1''$ nails, drilling the holes in the strip first if splitting seems likely. Note that the strip has a $15°$ bevel to obtain a better fit with the front of the box. A straight edge across the sides at point 'G' with a $\frac{3}{4}''$ spacer of scrap wood behind it will facilitate the strip's accurate placement prior to nailing.

Measure and mark the entrance hole location $6''$ up from the bottom on the centre line of the front, and note the requisite hole diameter (HD) for the bird you have selected. The entrance hole can be drilled neatly with a hole saw in a low speed drill press. For safety, be sure to clamp your work to the drill press table before starting to drill. Protect the drill press table with a flat piece of scrap plywood.

An expansion bit and hand brace also work well, should a drill press be unavailable. To avoid any danger of splitting the front when using this second method, turn it upside down and grip it across the top in the vise, above where the hole is to be drilled. Cut halfway through the front and then reverse it in the vise and complete the cut from the other side; this makes a neater hole and avoids the usual splitting out of wood on the exit side. Tidy up the hole, and break its edges using a sharp pocket knife and a half-round file.

Fit the front in position, making sure it is touching the roof, and clamp it across the front from side to side. Lightly tap two $2''$ finishing nails into the front through the pre-drilled swivel holes 'N' in the sides. Remove the

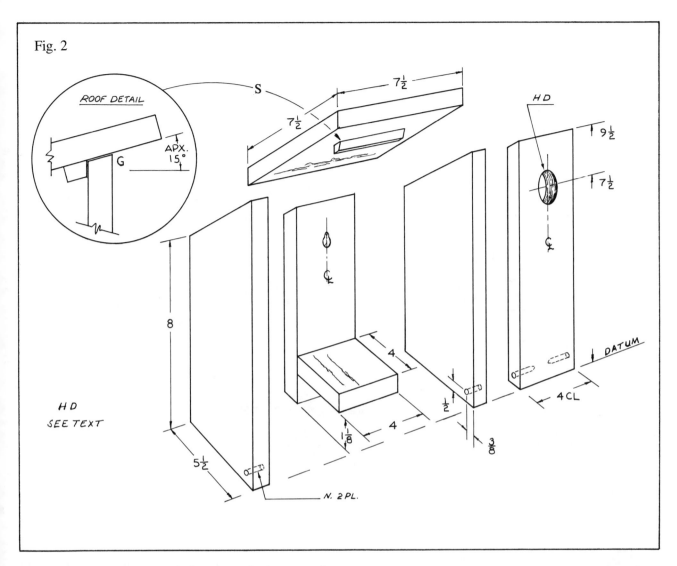

Fig. 2

ROOF DETAIL

APX. 15°

G

HD SEE TEXT

HD

DATUM

N. 2 PL.

front and pre-drill the two holes so marked accurately in the drill press using a small drill such as a $\frac{1}{16}''$ or less. It is easier and better to make this small guide-hole true and square in the drill press than it is simply to hammer the nails in and hope that they will be true, and that the wood won't split. Set the front in the box again and hammer the nails in; it is as well to leave them projecting about $\frac{3}{16}''$, so that they can be removed for adjustment or replacement.

Make two of the fastening pins shown in Figs. 15 and 16 and incorporate them to hold the front in place.

BIRD NO.	BIRD NAME	H.D.(in.) (HOLE DIA.)
1	House Wren	1
2	Bewick's Wren	1¼
3	Carolina Wren	1½
4	Tufted Titmouse	1¼
5	Carolina Chickadee	1¼
6	Black Capped Chickadee	1¼
7	Red Breasted Nuthatch	1¼

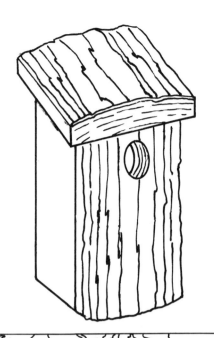

SECTION 2

The box shown in Fig. 3, although nominally for only two species, could easily be used by one of those listed in section 1, should such a bird feel so inclined. See photo 6, p. 58 for a similar box with a spring held lower front.

(8) WHITE BREASTED NUTHATCH

A slightly larger version of the Red Breasted Nuthatch, equally acrobatic but preferring deciduous woodlands to evergreen bush.

NEST SITE: Some eight to fifteen feet up, in deciduous bush, unsprayed orchards and trees in small communities. Leave an inch or two of detritus, wood shavings, pine needles, dead grass, or similar material on the box floor to encourage nesting.

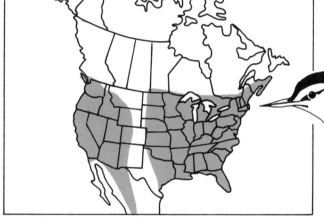

(9) DOWNY WOODPECKER

RANGE: Most of the USA and southern Canada coast to coast.

This small woodpecker is reasonably common over its range and feeds largely on insects and woodboring grubs, which are harmful to man's interests. It will take suet at a feeder, but is shyer than a chickadee. The nest box entrance hole diameter is often given as 1¼″, but as with other species, one or two subspecies vary a little in size, so a hole diameter of 1½″ is a safer bet, except that it allows entry to the House Sparrow.

NEST SITE: Some eight to fifteen feet up in evergreen, deciduous or mixed bush, unsprayed orchards and suburban shade trees. Cover the box floor with an inch or two of fine wood shavings or small chips to encourage nesting and as a bed for the eggs.

CONSTRUCTION

First cut out the pieces accurately; include some ventilation as shown in Figs. 4 and 5, and sand them smooth, as necessary. The keyhole is typically two merged holes $\frac{3}{16}''$ and $\frac{7}{16}''$ in diameter and is placed centrally some $1\frac{1}{2}''$ from the top of the back. A plain top is optional, but a bark slab top matches up better with the one piece bark slab front, which should be cut out now, but completed later.

Unlike the box in Section 1, the top of this one slopes down from the back, which extends 2″ below the floor of the box to accept an additional nail, if required, for steadying purposes. This provision is very useful, in view of the length of the box and its relatively high placement up a dead tree or pole.

Fit the sides up to the back, levelling them at the top and hammer in $1\frac{3}{4}''$ or 2″ common nails at 3 points, roughly $1\frac{1}{2}''$, 5″ and 9″ down from the top and $\frac{3}{8}''$ in from the rear edge of the side. Fit the floor between the sides level with their bottom edge, clamp it crosswise, and set two nails into it from the back. Put two more nails, one through each side, into the floor about $\frac{3}{4}''$ from the front edge.

Use six more 2″ spiral flat head nails to fasten down the roof. Line the roof up carefully and symmetrically at the back, and hammer two 2″ nails through it into the back of the box. Ensure that the front edges of the sides are parallel, and that the sides are at 90° to the back; then complete nailing down the roof using two nails in each side.

Mark out the entrance hole location $7\frac{1}{2}''$ up on the centre line of the inside surface of the front. To avoid splitting, clamp the front in the vise and complete the cut from the bark side to avoid splitting on the exit side. Clean up the hole with a sharp pocket knife and a coarse half-round file. A hole saw in a slow speed drill press also works well. Again, remember to clamp such work to the drill-press table before commencing to drill.

Cut the exit ladder slots into the inside surface of the front, as shown in Fig. 8, from the hole down to about 2″ above the floor. It is feasible to lower the front onto the saw blade and only cut the requisite, short, central steps, but most people will simply run the slots fully across from side to side. Drafts are likely with this method, and so the ends of such slots should be plugged with plastic wood, or other wood filler, for about 1″ from each side, the filler being sanded flush when dry.

Make up and fit the two $\frac{1}{2}''\times\frac{3}{8}''$ strips and nail and glue them to the inside of the front. This is best done by measurement and using partially driven 1″ nails, which allow adjustment of the strip until the correct position is found; the glue is then applied and the nails driven fully down. Allowance must be made at the lower end of the strip, so that the front can be removed easily, bottom first.

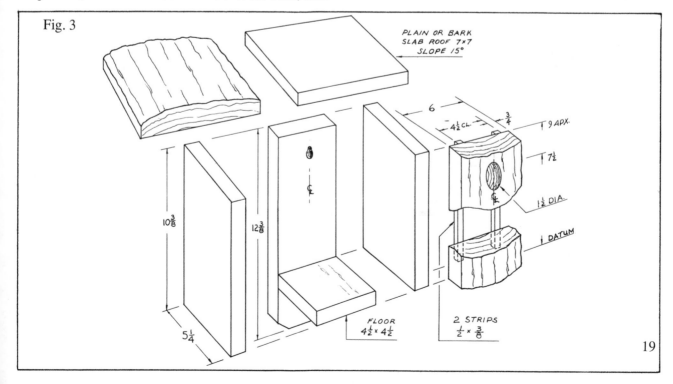

Fig. 3

PLAIN OR BARK
SLAB ROOF 7×7
SLOPE 15°

$10\frac{3}{8}$

$12\frac{3}{8}$

$5\frac{1}{4}$

FLOOR
$4\frac{1}{2} \times 4\frac{1}{2}$

2 STRIPS
$\frac{1}{2} \times \frac{3}{8}$

6

$4\frac{1}{2}$ CL.

$\frac{3}{4}$

9 APX.

$7\frac{1}{2}$

$1\frac{1}{2}$ DIA.

DATUM

19

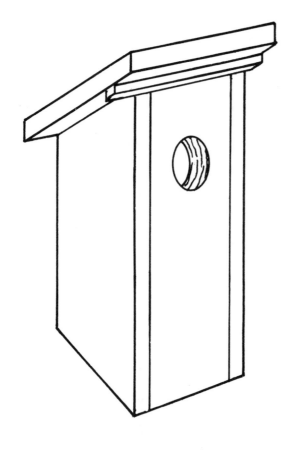

SECTION 3

The box shown in Fig. 4 is of a versatile design which may well attract the birds of Sections 1 and 2 as well as those of this section, assuming satisfactory siting. See also Fig. 60, for a similar, but combined nesting-roosting box.

(10) TREE SWALLOW

Like all the swallows, Tree Swallows are very good characters to have around. And like that champion flier, the Arctic Tern, they seem to be made to fly forever, and all the time they are flying, they are eating mosquitoes and other aerial pests by the thousands. I love to see them return in spring to nest in boxes made to the design of Fig. 4 in which they nested the previous year. I mention this because the entrance hole is somewhat higher than is generally recommended for these birds. The high hole may attract other species, perhaps a Bluebird, and it certainly provides a measure of protection against predators which is totally absent from a box with a lower hole.

Tree Swallows line their root-and-grass nests with feathers, and they will almost take these from your fingers as you release them in the wind. Their nests, however, soon become very foul; it is as well to sprinkle two or three tablespoons of diatomaceous earth under a Tree Swallow's nest to keep parasites away if trouble threatens.

As mentioned previously, House Sparrows can be a problem with any box they can enter, that is, one with a 1½″ diameter hole; these pests may have to be dealt with. The swallows soon catch on as to whose side you are on, however, and will keep trying for the box.

NEST SITE: Preferably in the vicinity of open or sparsely treed swamp, or moist areas where flying insects breed. The birds range over a wide and communal area, however, and will nest within 100 feet, and in sight, of each other. Boxes so set up, 6 to 10 feet up, in the open, are very well received. Boxes on catproof poles, away from dense brush, are taken in preference to boxes on tree trunks.

(11) BLUEBIRD

The quiet burbling of this winsome bird always catches a bird watcher's attention, for, like most other birds, it is not nearly as common as it once was. Modern steel T bars replace the former old wooden cedar fenceposts in which it used to nest, and agricultural pesticides have poisoned its food. Bluebirds still frequent old untended, unsprayed orchards, open woodlands and roadsides where natural cavities or manmade boxes are available. Their nests are left much cleaner than those of the swallow tribe.

NEST SITE: From five to seven feet up on or near a higher pole (say 15′), a wire or dead tree, from which the bird can descend to pick grubs and insects from your (hopefully unsprayed) lawn. Trees may be nearby, but bluebirds nest in the open, like the Tree Swallows which vie with them for nest boxes. House Wrens and House Sparrows may also cause them problems, but a box only five feet up appeals much more to a bluebird than to a House Sparrow.

The map shows, approximately, the combined ranges of both Eastern & Western Bluebirds.

CEDAR SIDING

CONSTRUCTION

Although of tapered section, cedar house-siding is an excellent substitute for the sides of the box as drawn. As cedar splits more easily than say, pine, or fir, a little more care might be necessary with the nailing.

Decide on your box height and cut out the pieces carefully; include the requisite ventilation in the floor and sides. The keyhole, as usual, is a $\frac{3}{16}''$ and $\frac{7}{16}''$ hole merged together by the use of, say, a coarse rat-tail file; it is located centrally about $1\frac{1}{2}''$ below the top of the back. The roof should have a rain slot, as shown in Fig. 5, roof detail.

Nail the floor to the back with two 2″ ring or spiral flat-head nails; these nails should not pass through any vent holes as this would promote premature rusting.

Now line up the sides against the back, level at the top, and nail them in position. The nails should be ⅜″ from the rear edge, about an inch from the top and bottom edges.

Line up the roof with the top of the back, with equal overhangs at each side, and nail it to the back. Check that the front edges of the sides are parallel and that the roof overhangs are equal, and drive four more nails through the roof into the sides.

The entrance hole on the centre line of the front will be either 6″ up from the bottom for a Tree Swallow or 7″up for a bluebird. Indent this position with an awl, set the box upside down in the vise and cut a 1½″ diameter hole with an expansion bit and hand brace. Cut the hole half way through and then reverse the front and finish the hole from the other side. Tidy up the hole with a sharp pocket knife and a coarse half-round file.

Cut the exit ladder, as shown in Fig. 8, into the inside surface of the front; there is no need to fill the ends of the ⅛″ cuts, as in Section 2, because the door is recessed and so is relatively draftproof.

Make and fit the upper retaining strip, say

¾″×½″×9½″, to the front of the roof. It does not have to go fully across the width of the roof but a longer strip will not split as easily as a short one. It looks well if the ends are chamfered upwards at 45 degrees, or you may wish to use the configuration of Fig. 1 (c) which is also excellent.

Cut the lower retaining strip, ½″×⅜″, to a length which will just pass between the sides and partially nail it, by measurement, to the front. Adjust it as required until the front fits closely but can be removed without undue force, then apply glue and nail it down fully; two 1″ nails are adequate.

Make a hook catch as shown in Figs. 20 to 23 and install it on the bottom of the box floor, as shown in Fig. 18. The hook shown in Fig. 19 is also good, but the Fig. 18 type is preferable because it is entirely under the box and so is protected. The forward projecting type in Fig. 19 is more liable to be pushed open either accidentally, or by a predator.

See photos 1 and 2, page 6 for photographs of the finished box and typical installations.

BIRD NO.	BIRD NAME	B.H.(in.) (BACK HEIGHT)	F.H.(in.) (FRONT HEIGHT)	H.H.(in.) (HOLE HEIGHT)
10	Tree Swallow	6¼(apx.)	8	6
11	Bluebird	7¼(apx.)	9	7

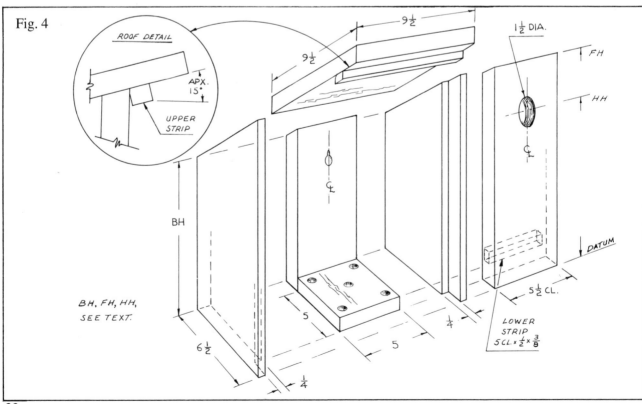

Fig. 4

ROOF DETAIL

APX. 15°

UPPER STRIP

9½

9½

1½ DIA.

FH

HH

C L

BH

BH, FH, HH, SEE TEXT.

DATUM

5½ CL.

LOWER STRIP
5CL.×½×⅜

5

5

6½

¼

¼

SECTION 4

The box shown in Fig. 5 is intended for hosting at least five species of birds which are all bigger than those considered in Sections 1 to 3. Although the smaller birds listed in these Sections might conceivably use this larger box, if vacant, they could hardly compete for it on equal terms with the birds listed in this section.

(12) GREAT CRESTED FLYCATCHER

This is a vigorous, excellent character to have around a garden, an old orchard or farm. The bird's diet is almost solely insects, grubs and caterpillars which we would rather do without. The nest may be in a natural cavity, a mail or newspaper box, or a nest box, and sometimes has a cast-off snakeskin included in its structure. House Sparrows are more of a problem for smaller birds, but the Starling is a very tough competitor for any box with an entrance hole 1¾″ or more in diameter which includes that of the Great Crested Flycatcher.

NEST SITE: Some eight to twenty feet up, in or close to deciduous or mixed bush.

(13) HAIRY WOODPECKER

Somewhat like a lively overgrown Downy Woodpecker, this quite impressive bird always commands a birdwatcher's attention. As it eats mostly wood-boring grubs and larvae, it helps to preserve the trees in which it lives. It is somewhat wary, but will come to a feeder for suet whilst not being dependent upon it as an essential food source.

Starlings are probably the worst pest that afflicts nest boxes which they can enter — those with holes 1¾″ or more in diameter, and conflicts can be expected between them and the Hairy Woodpecker.

NEST SITE: About five to twenty feet up, in mature deciduous or mixed bush, preferably far enough from buildings to avoid starlings finding the box. Always leave a few inches of small woodchips or fine shavings in the nest box to encourage nesting, as woodpeckers do not usually carry in any nest building materials, and a soft bed is needed for the eggs to rest on.

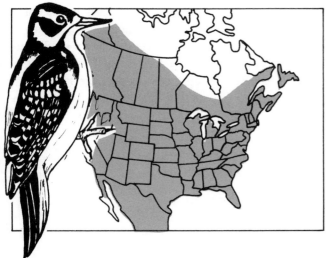

(14) RED-HEADED WOODPECKER

Roughly the same size as the Hairy, the Red-Headed Woodpecker is not common anywhere and a bird-watcher goes home happy after seeing one. Locally, the Red-Headed may add a little of man's corn to its usual diet of nuts and harmful grubs and insects. It is not above taking eggs and young of other birds on occasion. When present, starlings will provide competition for the holes available.

NEST SITE: Generally at a height of six to fifteen feet in open deciduous woodland, dead trees in burned areas, poles, and so on. Leave a few inches of small wood shavings or fine chips on the nest box floor, as woodpeckers do not generally carry any nesting materials into their nest holes.

(15) RED-BELLIED WOODPECKER

Similar in size to the Hairy Woodpecker, the Red-Bellied Woodpecker eats insects and grubs which man is glad to lose. Wild fruit is favoured as a dessert, but when the trees on which it grows have been replaced by, say, an orchard or orange grove, an orange or two may serve instead — which man is not glad to lose. As with other woodpeckers, starlings, when present, will compete for nesting holes.

NEST SITE: In evergreen or mixed bush, in dead pines or deciduous trees, orchards, plantations, etc. At a height of eight to twenty feet. Leave a few inches of small wood chips or shavings, pine needles, etc. in the bottom of the box to receive the eggs, as woodpeckers do not carry such materials into their nest holes.

(16) NORTHERN SAW-WHET OWL

A small but desirable owl to have in a woodlot, to which it may or may not return in successive years, being somewhat of a nomad. Its main diet is mice and other small rodents, and it also eats insects.

NEST SITE: In evergreen bush, ten to twenty feet up in a pine or spruce tree, preferably with dense thickets or dense younger evergreens nearby to provide cover and a place to roost during the day. Leave a few inches of small wood chips or shavings on the floor of the box to form a soft bed for the eggs and so encourage nesting.

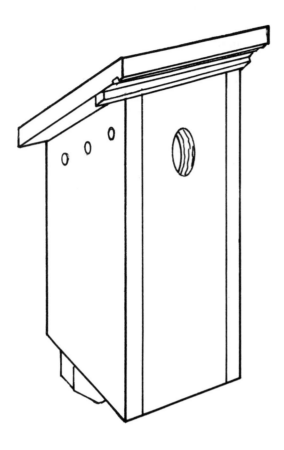

CONSTRUCTION

From the data given in Fig.5, determine the measurements for your intended tenants, and cut out the requisite pieces carefully. Note that, as it extends below the floor, the back for bird (12) is 11″, and for birds (13) to (16), it is 15″ in total length. This is mentioned because lengthening a piece of wood is a lot harder than shortening it.

The side vent holes should be about ⅜″ in diameter , and 4 or 5 similar holes may be drilled in the floor instead of the chamfered corners shown; see Figs. 4 and 5. The keyhole is a ³⁄₁₆″ hole and a ⁷⁄₁₆″ hole merged together about 1½″ down from the top of the back of the centre line.

Cut a rain slot in the roof like that of Fig. 5 roof detail, and sand all the pieces reasonably smooth, including their edges.

Make the two ¾″×½″ side strips shown in Fig. 5; they run down each side from the roof to within about 2″ of the floor. They steady the front and also reduce drafts. Position one parallel to the front edge of each side and ¾″ from it and then glue and nail them securely.

Line up the sides against the back, level at the top, and nail them in place. The nails should be on a line ⅜″ from the edge and roughly 1″, 4″ and 7″ down from the top of the box for bird No. (12) and at about 1″, 6″, and 11″ down for the box of birds (13) to (16).

Fit the floor into place level with the bottom edges of the sides, and clamp it crosswise so that it cannot move. Rest the front edge of the floor on a small block of wood and drive two nails through the back into the floor; this method will ensure that no floor-to-back gap occurs. Put four more nails, two through each side, into the floor, roughly 1½″ and 4″ from the front edge.

Six more 2″ spiral flat-head nails are now used to fasten down the roof. Line the roof up carefully with the back, with equal overhangs at each side, and hammer two nails through the roof into the back of the box. Ensure that the front edges of the sides are sensibly parallel, and that the roof overhangs them equally, and then use two nails on each side to secure the roof in position. This procedure takes care of any slight warps and makes for a box which is square and true with no gaps in it.

Mark out the entrance hole location on the centre line of the front; it will be 7″ up from the bottom for bird No. (12) and 11″ up for birds (13) to (16). Indent this position with an awl, and set the front upside down in the vise to stop it from splitting when you cut out the entrance hole. The hole will be 2″ in diameter for birds (12) to (15) and 2½″ in diameter for bird (16). Cut the chosen hole about halfway through with an expansion bit and a hand brace, and then reverse the wood and finish the hole from the other side, this obviating any break-out on the exit side of the hole. Clean up the hole with a sharp pocket knife and a coarse half-round file. A hole saw in a slow speed drill press also works well; for safety reasons, of course, such work should always be clamped down beforehand.

Cut out the exit ladder on the inside of the front (see Fig. 8); as the front is recessed, these cuts may run fully across the front, without any need to fill their ends.

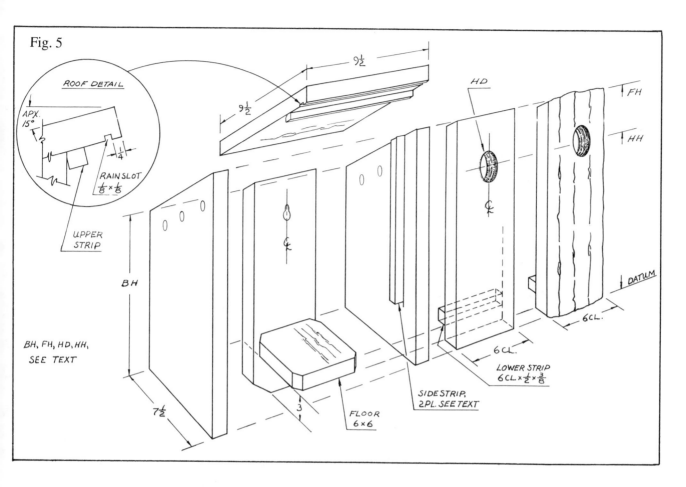

Fig. 5

ROOF DETAIL

APX. 15°

RAIN SLOT ⅛ × ⅛

UPPER STRIP

9½

9½

HD

FH

HH

BH

BH, FH, HD, HH, SEE TEXT

7½

3

FLOOR 6×6

SIDE STRIP, 2 PL. SEE TEXT

6CL.

6CL.

LOWER STRIP 6CL × ½ × ⅜

6CL.

DATUM

Make the upper strip, say 9½″×¾″×½″, as shown in Fig 5 roof detail, and with the front in place, glue and nail it to the roof. The strip may be shorter than 9½″, if desired, and it may be necessary to remove some bark and make a suitable flat for it to seat against, if a bark front is used.

Now make a lower strip ½″×⅜″ and slightly less than 6″ long, and set it in place on the inside of the front, ¾″ up from the bottom, with three partially driven nails. Try removing and replacing the front, adjust the lower strip accordingly, and then glue and nail it in its final position. The front should then come off easily, bottom first.

Make up a hook catch as shown in Figs. 20 to 23 and install it underneath the box as shown in Fig. 18.

BIRD NO.	BIRD NAME	B.H.*(in.) (BACK HEIGHT)	F.H.(in.) (FRONT HEIGHT)	H.D.(in.) (HOLE DIA.)	H.H.(in.) (HOLE HEIGHT)
12	Great Crested Flycatcher	8*	10	2	7
13	Hairy Woodpecker	12*	14	2¼	11
14	Red-Headed Woodpecker	12*	14	2¼	11
15	Red-Bellied Woodpecker	12*	14	2¼	11
16	Northern Saw-Whet Owl	12*	14	2½	11

* See construction notes on page 26 before cutting.

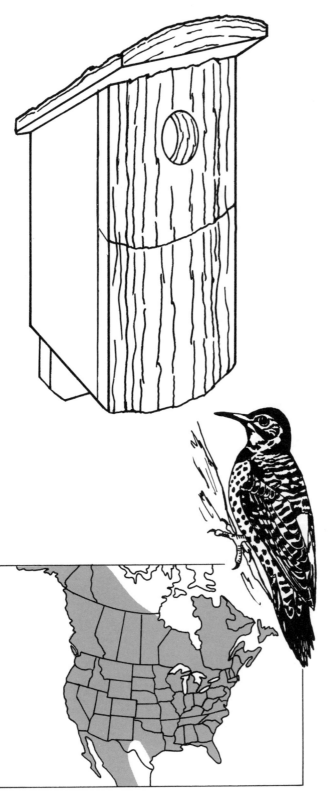

SECTION 5

The box shown in Fig. 6 may be used by the birds of Section 5, but such birds could not prevail against the American Kestrel or Screech-Owl (Eastern and Western) should either want the nesting cavity. See Fig 6 and photos 5 and 6 on pages 57 & 58 for an idea of the finished box.

(17) NORTHERN FLICKER

The name refers to two species, formerly known as the Yellow Shafted Flicker and the Red Shafted Flicker.

Flickers are very good birds to have around the woodlot or the lawn; in the latter they frequently prospect for the grass-damaging white larvae of the June beetle, cutworms and other pests. Wild fruits are preferred to man's cultivated varieties. Although they are quite large, vigorous woodpeckers, Flickers are somewhat meek, and tend to allow starlings, which are much smaller but far more aggressive, to dispossess them of their nesting holes. They therefore need our assistance in that respect, if they are to retain their numbers.

NEST SITE: Usually four to twenty feet up a tree, often a dead one, in a cavity which they have hollowed out or enlarged. The site may be near a swamp or in deciduous, evergreen or mixed bush, frequently near open areas which offer explorations on the ground. The box is best sited in open bush, away from buildings which may attract starlings. Like most woodpeckers, Flickers are not noted for carrying materials into their nesting cavities, so it is necessary to leave a few inches of small wood chips, shavings, pine needles, etc. on the box floor, as a soft bed for the eggs which you hope they will lay.

(18) AMERICAN KESTREL
(FORMERLY KNOWN AS THE SPARROW HAWK)

Commonly seen on hydro poles and wires by roadsides, or hovering over a field in search of mice, grasshoppers, crickets, and other insects injurious to man's endeavours. Migrates to the southern parts of its range in winter, but is in no hurry to leave its breeding areas.

NEST SITE: Often in a dead tree in an unused woodpecker hole, fifteen to twenty-five feet up, in open country. A few inches of small wood chips or shavings should be left in the nest box to simulate the floor of a natural cavity. I prefer not to encourage it near other nest boxes, however, as it has been known to kill small birds for food, chiefly in the nesting season to feed its young.

(19) SCREECH OWL
(EASTERN AND WESTERN)

Somewhat like a nocturnal counterpart of the American Kestrel, the Screech Owl's diet is largely made up of small rodents and a wide range of insects injurious to man's objectives. As it also takes a few birds, chiefly in winter or when breeding, it is well not to encourage it to nest near the nest boxes of smaller and less aggressive birds.

NEST SITE: Unused woodpecker holes, or natural cavities, ten to twenty-five feet up, in evergreen or mixed bush. A few inches of pine needles, small wood chips or shavings should cover the floor of the nest box, to simulate natural conditions.

The map shows, approximately, the combined ranges of both Eastern & Western Screech Owls.

29

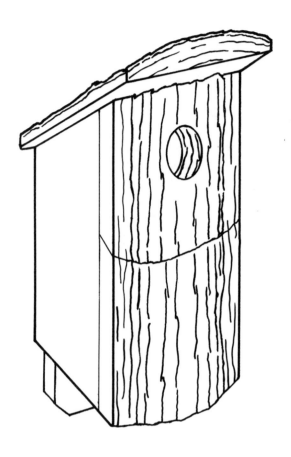

CONSTRUCTION

Making the box of Fig. 6 is straightforward, as the dimensions do not vary for the three species under consideration. Bark slabs tend to make it a little less conspicuous, but plain wood is not ruled out as an alternative.

Cut out all the pieces accurately, noting that the back, at 16″, is longer than the sides. Extending the back below the floor allows the use of an additional nail to steady the box which could otherwise be disturbed by a high wind or a predator. The chamfered corners shown on the extension are optional, but make for a tidier appearance; they measure roughly 1″×1″.

Drill a few ½″ diameter ventilation holes in the sides

and floor, as shown in Figs. 4 and 5, and make a keyhole by merging a ³⁄₁₆″ hole and a ⁷⁄₁₆″ hole on the centre line of the back, about 2″ from the top. Cut a rain slot in the roof as shown in the roof detail of Fig. 5.

Cut out the 3″ diameter entrance hole in the slab front, 12″ up from the bottom on the centre line. This can be done with a hole saw in a slow speed drill press, the front being clamped to the table for safety reasons; do not omit this precaution. Another way is to clamp the front upside down in the vise and cut out the hole with a hand brace and an expansion bit. Drill halfway through the front and then reverse it and complete the cut from the other side. The vise stops the front from splitting, and so makes for a neater hole.

Using a table saw (you could use a hand saw), cut the exit ladder as shown in Fig. 8. If you run the cuts fully across the board, fill them in with wood filler for an inch at each end, to prevent drafts, and then sand them level when dry. Now saw the front across at 45 degrees as shown in Fig. 6; sand all the pieces, including their edges, relatively smooth; and assemble them with 2″ flat-head spiral nails, as follows:

Line up the sides against the back, level at the top, and nail them together. The nails will be on a line ³⁄₈″ from the edge, roughly 1″, 4½″, 8½″ and 12″ from the bottom. This spacing prevents any conflict with the nails holding the roof and floor.

Fit the floor in place, level with the bottom edges of the sides and clamp it securely, cross-wise. Measure and draw the centre line of the floor on the back, rest the front edge of the floor on a small wooden block, and drive two nails through the back into the floor. This method avoids any small gaps between the floor and the back. Drive three more nails through each side into the bottom; these will be on a line ³⁄₈″ from the bottom edge and some 1″, 3″ and 6½″ from the front.

Drill three nail clearance holes with, say, a ³⁄₃₂″ drill, in each side of the fixed top section of the front, on a line ³⁄₈″ from each side and approximately 1½″, 4″ and 7″ down from the top. These six holes are best drilled from the bark side on a drill press, having been first marked out and indented with an awl. Set the drilled top section in position, aligned with the front edges and tops of the sides and nail it in place.

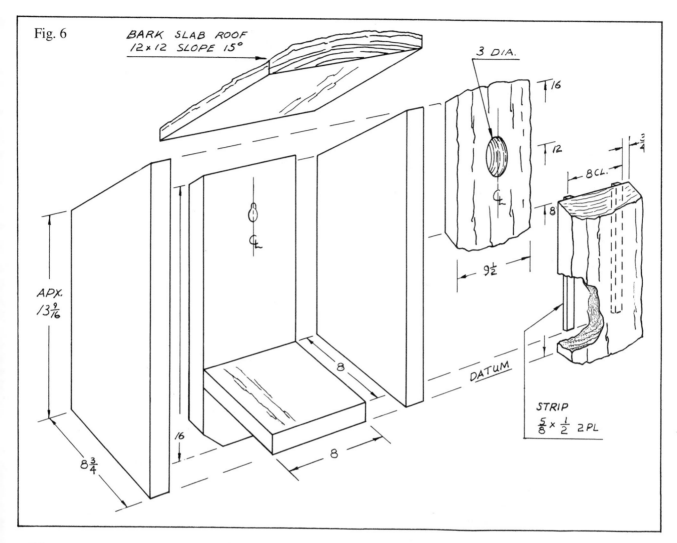

Fig. 6

BARK SLAB ROOF
12 × 12 SLOPE 15°

3 DIA.

APX. 13 9/16

8 3/4

16

8

8

9½

DATUM

STRIP
5/8 × 1/2 2 PL

Line up the roof with the back of the box, with equal overhangs at both sides, and nail it down, using three nails at each side and two more nails, longer ones if necessary, at the back. Support the lower edge of the fixed front and hammer two more nails through the top into it.

Make the two front retaining strips (see Fig. 6). They measure some 7¼″ long by approximately ⅝″×½″ and prevent any sideways or downward movement of the front; they also prevent drafts. Partially nail them to the back of the lower, removable front, ¾″ from each edge. Try the front for fit, and adjust or trim the retainer strips until a satisfactory fit is obtained; the top is pushed in top first, and bottom last.

A very convenient way of holding the front on is with two springs, as shown in Fig. 24 and photo 6. For access, the bottom of the front is pulled outwards to clear the strips, and the front is then slid under the box, as shown, in photo 7. As the box may be placed fairly high up, perhaps necessitating climbing, this arrangement is of value because it obviates accidentally dropping the front; also, it is feasible to open it with one hand. If additional security is required, (for example, a spring might rust and break) a hook catch such as that in Fig. 18 may also be added. The two springs should be greased and protected by moulding as shown in Fig. 24 and photo 5, in which case they generally last many years.

SECTION 6

The box shown in Fig. 7 is intended to be nailed to a pole or a dead tree. If a steel pipe is to hold up the box over water — see Fig. 12 — it would be advantageous to use a box similar to that of Fig. 6, but with the dimensions increased accordingly. These two boxes will be referred to as type A and type B respectively. Weight would be minimized by substituting plain wood for the bark slabs; the Fig. 6 type of roof would also save on weight, as Fig. 1(b) illustrates. Cutting down on weight is important in large boxes, particularly if the somewhat heavier exterior grade plywood is used in their construction. The internal keyhole mounting is not altogether suitable for these large boxes; it is better to see the nail, in case it sags downwards. Also, if it projected much inside the box, it could easily harm the Wood Duck, which often enters at some speed.

(20) WOOD DUCK

A beautifully coloured duck with a liking for trees and wooded areas. The diet includes insects, aquatic vegetation, acorns and small creatures such as frogs.

NEST SITE: In open woodland bordering swamps, streams and ponds, from five feet (over water) to twenty feet up in a hollow tree or dead stump, sometimes at a surprisingly long distance from water.

Wood duck nesting boxes are often seen on poles driven into the mud of the reedy shallows which border lakes and rivers. These boxes are set up by conservationists to encourage breeding and increase numbers. Many such "conservationists" are duck hunting club members and there is raging controversy over their role in helping or hindering duck populations. No doubt the situation would be much worse if duck clubs did not 'raise their own birds' as it were.

Golden Eye and Bufflehead ducks also nest in cavities, and have been known to use nesting boxes.

To simulate the natural cavities used by these ducks, it is necessary to put a few inches of shavings, small wood chips, or other semi-resilient matter on the floor of the nesting box. Most birds do not like to lay their eggs on a hard, flat board, and ducks do not seem to like to carry much in the way of nesting material into boxes.

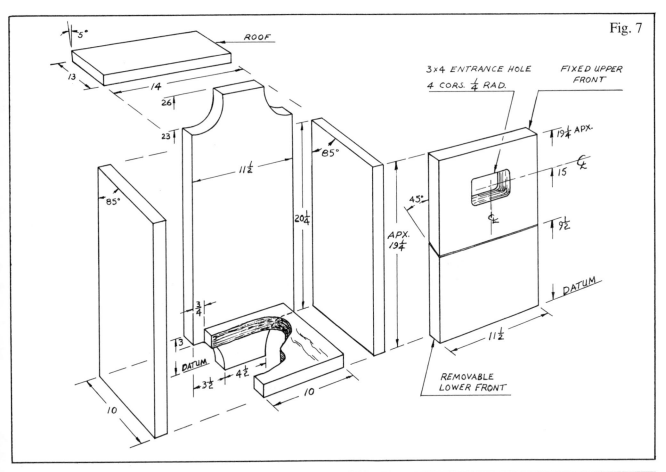

Fig. 7

ROOF

5°

13

14

26

23

11½

85°

85°

20¼

¾

3

DATUM

3½ 4½

10

DATUM

10

3×4 ENTRANCE HOLE
4 CORS. ¼ RAD.

FIXED UPPER FRONT

19¼ APX.

15 ℄

9½

45°

APX. 19¼

11½

REMOVABLE LOWER FRONT

CONSTRUCTION

Cut out the pieces accurately to the dimensions given in Fig. 7. Note that the back is 26″ long; the curves at its top and bottom are detailed in Figs. 9 and 10. These curves enhance the appearance of the box, but a simple bevel, as suggested by the dotted lines in Fig. 10, is easier to cut and also looks well. Extending the back below the floor allows the box to be steadied by a second nail or clamp.

Drill several ½″ ventilation holes in the sides and floor as shown in Figs. 4 and 5. As this is a large box, it calls for about twice as many holes as those shown. Although ducks are noted for being watertight, a flooded nest hardly helps them to incubate their eggs, so it is fortunate that the holes in the floor also provide drainage when needed.

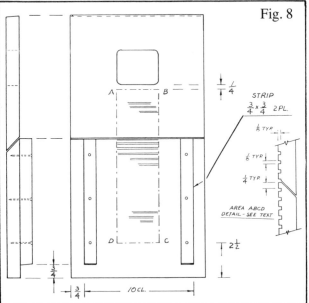

Fig. 8

A   B

¼

STRIP
¾ × ¾ 2 PL.

⅙ TYP.

⅙ TYP.

¼ TYP.

AREA ABCD
DETAIL - SEE TEXT

D   C

2½

¾

¾

10 CL.

Mark out the 3″×4″ entrance hole on the front and radius of four corners by drilling them first with a ½″ drill. These four holes should be marked out ¼″ inside the two lines forming the corners, and indented with an awl. The four holes are then joined by chain drilling just inside the outline or using a keyhole or sabre saw. When the hole is cut, smooth the edge all around it with a coarse file and some sandpaper.

Cut the exit ladder slots into the inside surface of the front (Fig. 8). Running the cuts fully across the front will necessitate filling their ends to stop drafts, so it is better to make shorter cuts. This can be done by clamping two travel-limiting boards to the saw table, and sawing the cuts out by sliding the front along the fence from one to the other. The fence is adjusted in increments of ⅜″, and each cut is made by resting one edge of the front against the limit board on the feed side, and slowly lowering it onto the blade; it is then slid along to the other limit board to give cuts of approximately 4″ long. This method is sound and workable for the shallow ⅛″ deep cuts required, but is not to be recommended for deeper cuts. Saw the front in half at 45 degrees, as shown in Fig. 7.

An alternative to cutting slots is to nail a 4″ strip of cast-off carpeting to the front; this may not endure well, however. Close mesh chicken wire is not to be recommended for a ladder, as a nestling might become entangled in it or injured on sharp ends when the netting rusts out and breaks up. Although a cut ladder takes a little more time to make, it occupies no room, requires no maintenance, and lasts as long as the box.

Before assembling the box, use a piece of scrap brass or steel, such as the cover of an electrical junction box, to make and fit a supporting strip (Fig. 9), or the rather more suitable keyhole plate shown in Fig. 10. The two no. 8 – ¾″ screws in the strip are 2″ apart, and in the plate they are 2″ apart horizontally and ¾″ vertically. The keyhole itself is a ¼″ hole and a ½″ hole merged together with a rat-tail file; the centre lines of the strip and the plate are respectively 2″ and 1¾″ above the shoulder level.

Line up each side in turn along the edges of the back with their lower edges level with the bottom shoulder and nail them in place through the back, using 2″ flat-head spiral nails. Set the nails on a line ⅜″ from the edge of the back and roughly 1″, 5″, 9″, 13″, 17″ and 21″ up from the bottom.

Fit the floor in place, level with the bottom edge of the sides and clamp it firmly across the sides. Rest the front edge of the floor on a wooden block on the bench, and hammer three nails through the back into the floor. This method will ensure that there is no small gap between the floor and the back. Check that the front edge of the floor aligns with the sides and set three more nails through each side into the floor. These should be on a line ⅜″ up from the edge of the sides and about 1″, 4″ and 8″ from the front.

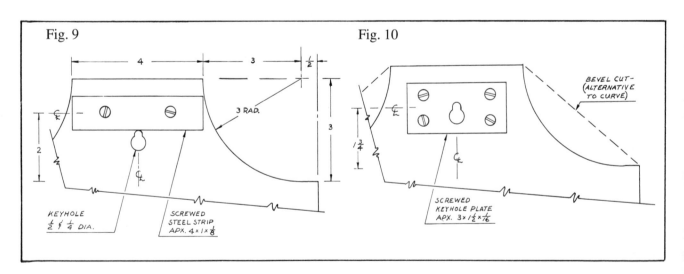

Fig. 9

Fig. 10

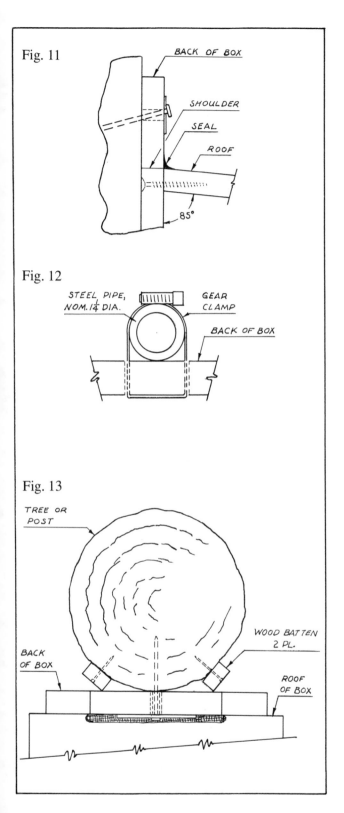

Fig. 11

BACK OF BOX
SHOULDER
SEAL
ROOF
85°

Fig. 12

STEEL PIPE, NOM. 1¼ DIA.
GEAR CLAMP
BACK OF BOX

Fig. 13

TREE OR POST
WOOD BATTEN 2 PL.
BACK OF BOX
ROOF OF BOX

Set the fixed upper front in place, aligning the sides with its edges, and use three nails on each side to secure it in place. If not already cut, the top edge of the front should now have its 5 degree bevel planed on, to enable the roof to fit correctly.

Put the roof on the box against the back with equal overhangs at the sides and screw it to the back. Check for equal overhangs at the front, and then nail the roof down, using roughly the same nail spacing as the sides. Support the lower edge of the front with a block of wood when nailing the roof to the front; this will prevent it from loosening.

Cut out the two vertical retaining strips shown in Fig. 8 and secure them to the removable lower front, ¾″ from the edges, so that the front can be installed and removed easily.

Install the two springs which secure the front, as shown in Fig. 24. These contraction springs should be roughly ⁵⁄₁₆″ in diameter, and made of ¹⁄₃₂″ diameter wire. When greased, and protected by moulding, as shown, they will last many years. If inspecting is infrequent for any reason, and in case a spring fractures, it is as well to make a pair, (L and R) of the hook catches shown in Fig. 18 and install them under the box as shown. When spaced about 4″ apart, 2″ each side of centre, and engaging outwards, they can simply be squeezed together for access and will clear the front when it is swung down.

Apply a fillet of durable sealant to the roof-to-back joint (Fig. 11).

For the alternative box (B) mentioned earlier, the dimensions are: BH = 17¼″, FH = 20″, HD = 3″×4″, HH = 15″ with a roof slope of approximately 15 degrees. The upper clamp is run through two slots in the back, in roughly the same place as the internal keyhole would be, some 2½″ down from the top. A similar clamp secures the bottom of the box through two more slots, or saw cuts, in the back where it extends below the floor. It is as well to check such clamps once a year or more often, and tighten them as necessary, should the wood dry out a little and so loosen them. The type (A) box, using two nails, requires two battens (or broken branches) to steady it as shown in Fig. 13. Plumber's metal strapping, bolted to the box with the nuts outside, may also be used to nail the box to a tree.

35

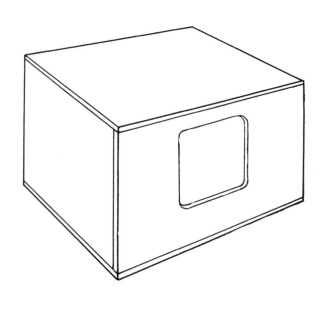

SECTION 7

The box shown in Fig. 14 is a modification of a design by Dr. Carl Marti of Odgen, Utah, and is made of ½″ exterior grade plywood. Thicker plywood would make a stronger box, but the extra weight would make the box harder to handle. The floor area and hole size are larger than those usually quoted, but Common Barn Owls are large birds, and their young need space around them as they grow. In fact, Dr. Marti finds that the bigger the box, the better the survival rate.

(21) COMMON BARN OWL

As the preferred diet of these owls is very largely rats and various mice, it thoroughly deserves its reputation as a farmer's friend. Wherever pesticides and poisoned baits are used, however, the owls eat the poisoned rats and also die painfully. As the name implies, barns are favoured nesting places, but as the older wooden structures are replaced by modern, tightly made aluminum sheds, the available nesting sites diminish in number — and so, unhappily, do the owls.

NEST SITE: Occasionally a few feet above ground but generally high up in a disused building, an abandoned silo or barn, or high up in a cavity in an old tree. The man-made structures used tend to be near farms and open fields, where the birds can hunt small rodents, but small marshes in open woodland also serve the same purpose.

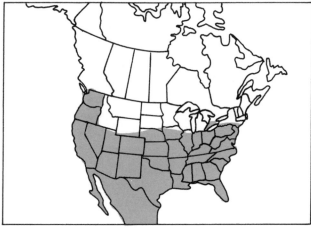

The box of Fig. 14 may be awkward to fasten in a tall tree without the aid of a natural branch formation in which to fasten it. Climbing and ropes would also be involved, so it is perhaps best to install the box in an abandoned silo or barn, high up, near the roof. Each installation will differ according to circumstances; for example, it may be feasible to cut an 8″ hole in the gable of the ruin and to set the box, with its own front removed, behind it. Or a 'built in' box can perhaps be made by allowing similar access to an existing corner of the roof, and adding a few well placed boards to form a nesting compartment.

Before encouraging owls to nest, it is vital to pick an area which is as free as possible from the types of chemical pollution most damaging to them. Sadly, such areas are becoming fewer and fewer, and this slow destruction of poison-free habitat costs us more and more birds, of all kinds, as it progresses each year.

For example, the risk of secondary poisoning is very high for owls and other raptors when rodenticides (the anticoagulant Warfarin is one such rat poison) or pigeon-sparrow-blackbirds poisons are used in the vicinity. Similarly, owls may pick up rodents that have been exposed to toxic insecticides, either by external contamination or internal poisoning. Those applied as granules are thought to be especially hazardous to raptors because of the potentially high levels that could accumulate in the guts of their prey.

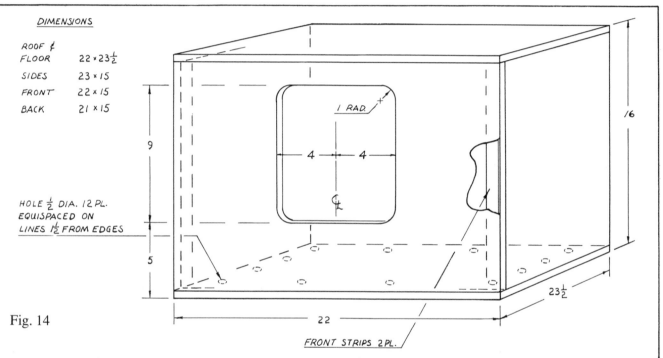

DIMENSIONS

ROOF & FLOOR	22 × 23½
SIDES	23 × 15
FRONT	22 × 15
BACK	21 × 15

HOLE ½ DIA. 12 PL. EQUISPACED ON LINES 1½ FROM EDGES

FRONT STRIPS 2 PL.

Fig. 14

CONSTRUCTION

Although large, the box is simple to build. Cut out the pieces carefully to the dimensions of the table in Fig. 14 and sand them reasonably smooth. Use a hole saw and a sabre saw to cut out the central entrance hole. Rounded corners look better and are stronger than sharp ones, but the radius is not critical and a hole saw smaller than the 2″ one called for may be used instead. Several ventilation/drainage holes are provided, as some of them may become plugged, particularly if placed centrally.

Nail the sides, back, roof and floor together with 1¾″ flat-head spiral nails, taking care to centre them in the thickness of the plywood to prevent splitting.

Cut two ¾″×¾″×15″ wooden strips and nail and glue one to each side of the front, ½″ from the edge as shown in Figs. 14 and 8, so that the front fits snugly in place.

Make four hook-catches, two left-handed and two right-handed, of the type shown in Fig. 18, and fit them, two on each side, to the box to secure the front. Nail the catches roughly 3″ and 12″ up from the floor and ensure that they open upwards.

CHAPTER 4.
NEST BOX ACCESSORIES & MISCELLANEOUS BIRD-AIDS

The construction details for making seven different bird boxes, and their variations, were given in Chapter 3. To avoid complications, I have illustrated the various box accessories such as fasteners and add-on holes separately. These items, and the way in which they can be made, are explained in this chapter. Nesting materials for birds in general, the bird watching scene, and the construction of bird shelves, are also covered.

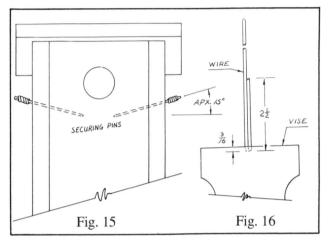

Fig. 15   Fig. 16

Fig. 15 shows a simple method of securing the down-swinging front of the type of box shown in Fig. 2 (p. 17). Two securing pins are used because if one is dropped in long grass, the other will hold the front closed until it, or a replacement, is found. This can prevent an unwanted exodus of young birds.

Securing pins can be wooden pegs, but these tend to swell and jam. The pins shown are made from our old friend coat hanger wire, and are quite simple and quick to make. A 180 degree closed bend of wire is set up tightly in the vise as shown in Fig. 16. The long end of the hairpin bend is then pushed firmly away from you, across the vise, and then wrapped tightly around the upright section to form a close coil of some five turns. The end loop in the vise should be as small as possible. Saw the free end off the coil and crimp up the last turn in the vise, making sure that the wire end is filed round and smooth to avoid cut fingers when withdrawing the pins. A #37, or possibly a $\frac{7}{64}''$ drill will suit most coat

hanger wire. Common $2\frac{1}{2}''$ nails may be used instead of the pins, but they are somewhat harder on the fingers. A #32 or #31 drill is adequate for them initially, with a $\frac{1}{8}''$ drill to follow if required. The heads of the nails must be deburred and smooth and should not project more than $\frac{1}{2}''$ from the sides of the box.

Note that the holes slope slightly downwards to prevent the pins from falling out. Initially a firm fit should be obtained, with later redrilling if swelling and jamming becomes a problem.

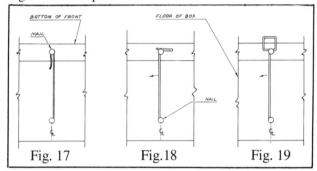

Fig. 17   Fig.18   Fig. 19

Figs. 17, 18 and 19 depict three simple ways of securing the lower end of the fronts of Figs. 3, 4 and 5. The fronts of these boxes slide into place upwards, top first; the bottom of the front is then pushed in to rest on its internal strips. The catch underneath the box is then swivelled to engage with the nail in the bottom edge of the front, thus securing it in place. This simple method uses no hinges and fulfils all the requisite parameters mentioned earlier; moreover, there are no detachable parts to lose.

Whoever made time made a lot of it, but for those who feel it is in short supply, two nails and a piece of bent wire will suffice as a catch (Fig. 17). For access, the wire is unhooked from the front nail; in time, of course, the wire will fatigue and break.

A better way, still using two nails, is to make a catch of coat hanger wire to the configurations of Fig. 18 or 19. Figs. 20 to 23 show how to make the hook-catch shown in Fig. 18. It is easily and quickly made with wire-bending pliers. If these are unavailable, a serviceable pair can be made by grinding down a broken pair of long-nosed pliers into tapering conical jaws.

Where several items, all alike, are required, it is better to use jig methods instead of pliers. Drive a 3½" nail into a piece of scrap 2"×4" wood at N in Fig. 20. Cut the head off, and wrap a loop of coat hanger wire around it; saw the wire along the dotted line, removing the shaded section. Flatten the loop with smooth pliers or in the vise, using protective brass chops to prevent scoring.

Drive in another nail at M in Fig. 21, 3" from N and bend the wire around it as shown. Apply a pair of long-nosed, or other ⅜" wide pliers, close to the plier joint, over the length L and bend up the free end of wire to form the shape shown in the vise jaws of Fig. 22. Close the jaws up tightly to the shape shown in the vise jaws of Fig. 23. Cut the free end off about ⅜" above the vise and hammer the remaining stub onto the fixed jaw, or the moveable jaw, of the vise according to whether you need a R.H. or L.H. hook catch. True-up the bends,

as need be, and deburr the end.

When cutting such wire, it is best to cut part way through, release the pressure, and then rotate the side cutters 90 degrees and complete the cut. This avoids the usual sharp edged ridge and so reduces deburring. The vise marks at the arrow of Fig. 22 are a bonus; they work like a ratchet and help to keep the hook closed. Finally, adjust the loop to accept a #8 round-headed wood screw.

Such custom-made hook catches cost next to nothing, and are more convenient to use than the store bought variety, which may or may not be available in the size required.

The catch of Fig. 19 is made in a way similar to the previous one, save that pliers are used to bend the rectangular hook end. From a safety point of view, the design of Fig. 18 is preferable.

Fig. 24 shows a two-section front which is handy for

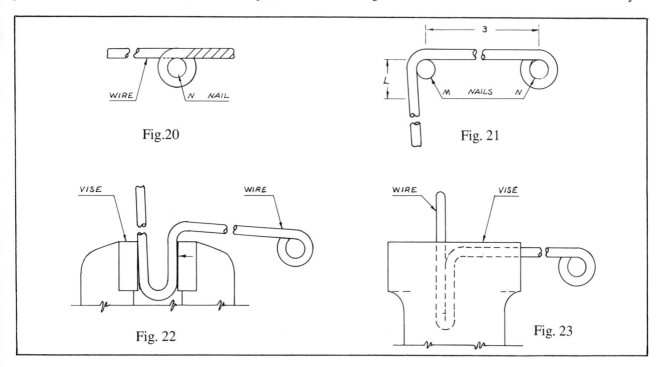

Fig.20

Fig. 21

Fig. 22

Fig. 23

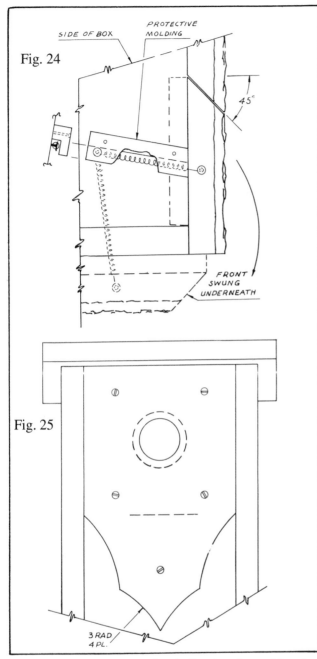

Fig. 24

Fig. 25

SIDE OF BOX

PROTECTIVE MOLDING

45°

FRONT SWUNG UNDERNEATH

3 RAD 4 PL.

directs any small drafts upwards away from the nestlings. Photo 7 shows the lower front in the open position, under the box. It is a very convenient arrangement with no detachable pieces to fall on the ground.

Fig. 25 depicts an add-on hole which can be used to reduce the entrance hole diameter, thus making a box versatile enough to suit differing species, as need arises. If, for example, there were no bluebird or Tree Swallow takers for your original 1½″ dia. entrance hole, you could reduce it to 1¼″ dia., and then install the box in cedar bush to try for chickadees.

The device can also be used to lengthen the entrance hole, retaining the original diameter, to make it more difficult for a predator to reach in. The add-on hole may be in ¼″ to ¾″ thick wood as required, and can be somewhat decorative, as shown in Fig. 25. It should be long enough for the birds to lever against with their tails when entering. A rectangular add-on, for example, cut along the dotted line, would make access difficult for them, and so should not be used. The add-on should not be installed inside the box as it would markedly reduce the available space and a short version therein would make it very difficult for the youngsters to climb out.

Add-on holes work best screwed to smooth, ¾″ finished lumber fronts. Bark slab fronts, being rough and uneven, do not lend themselves to add-ons, appearance-wise especially. Fortunately, their greater thickness makes entrance holes already long enough to discourage predators.

It is also feasible to reduce the size of a birdbox entrance hole by means of a turned wooden insert shaped like a serviette ring. This requires the use of a lathe and works best when glued into the hole permanently. As the wall of such a ring insert is only about ⅛″ to ¼″ thick, the device is relatively weak and likely to shrink. To obviate this, it is best to reduce the outside diameter of the middle third of the ring by about ¹⁄₁₆″, and wrap a few close turns of 0.02″ copper wire around it in the recess thus created. The turns are then soft soldered together. This strengthened insert will stand up better to temporary use, which may entail jamming it in place with masking tape, or some other strip-like packing, for the duration of the nesting season. Next time, it may be required for a different box.

large boxes. The top section is fixed and provides rigidity; the bottom section is held by two contraction springs, one on each side of the box. It is a good idea to shield them with L-section trim as this keeps rain off and avoids the possibility of birds getting their claws trapped between the coils. The 45 degree saw-cut between the top and bottom section of the front keeps rain out and

ATTRACTING BIRDS
IN GENERAL

A bird's basic needs seem to be freedom, cover, food, water and the company of its own kind, which last varies somewhat according to the season. It would seem then, that we should plant our available acreages with those shrubs and trees, including wild species, which bear the seeds, fruits, nuts and berries on which birds subsist. If it were more widespread, such a policy would enhance bird populations and possibly take some of the sting out of moving house - you might find an even better bird-haven than your old one.

NESTING MATERIALS

In terms of time and effort, nesting materials are the easiest of all bird-aids to make and install. The best material I have found is the coarse yellow twine used in agricultural binders. Very thin strips of cotton from an old sheet, strands of wool and light cotton-like string also have their advocates. CAUTION: regardless of the material, do not cut strips longer than 8″. Orioles have strangled themselves on fibres over 8″ long. Longer fibres, usually of grass, are admittedly used, but a bird in trouble might be able to break free from dried grass but not from the stronger man-made fibres.

The binder twine is first cut into lengths of seven to eight inches and then untwisted and teased out into groups of a few individual strands. Collect enough of these together to make up a loose bundle which measures an inch or so in diameter when restrained by a partially relaxed elastic band. Other natural fibres, as mentioned previously, may be mixed in with the binder twine, but muted colours are preferred over bright ones. It is a good idea to make up several bundles, to use as refills.

Fishing line and most other synthetic materials are unsuitable, as they are too wiry, strong and slippery for the birds to use. They will also not break down over time and can entangle birds. Natural materials such as cotton, hemp, and wool are by far the best.

A good way of offering this nesting material is to drive two 2½″ nails, about 1″ apart and side by side, into the side of an old fence post, about 2″ from the top. Fit one of the bundles between the nails and hold it in place with another band, multiple-wrapped back and forth across the nails. When mounted this way, strands of binder twine stay reasonably upright and are relatively easy for the birds to pull out. It is best to use several such stations, replacing the material as the supply is used up, or the bands perish. A mousetrap, nailed to the post, will also serve as a convenient holder of nesting material.

A few cavity nesters, Tree Swallows for example, will take a few strands to add to their usual dried-grass-and-roots mixture, but non cavity nesters will be your most frequent customers, which is the object of the exercise. The skilful female oriole undoubtedly makes the most ingenious use of these supply stations for weaving her amazing, hanging-pouch nest. Orioles live almost entirely on harmful insects of the tree-damaging variety, and the gorgeous male resembles a living orange flame as he runs up a tree branch in pursuit of a meal.

In addition to orioles, Cedar Waxwings, Great Crested Fly-catchers, American Robins and many other birds will entertain you as they work vigorously to loosen up the fibres they want. By observing the direction of a bird's departure, one can often locate its nest. To facilitate matters, perhaps it is as well to give the reader a few ideas on the rudiments of bird watching.

BIRD WATCHING

Not too many years ago, bird watchers were commonly thought to be mildly deranged and, as a civilized activity, bird watching grew only slowly. Today, however, its popularity bestows respectability on it as a valid pursuit for people of all ages; it has been described as the fastest growing hobby in North America.

Real enthusiasts drive to their favourite areas and often walk many miles, recording what they see, and where and when, and so on. Score cards are compared and tabulated jointly to arrive at bird population estimates, a very useful activity. Bird migrations bring seasonal gatherings of bird watchers to known bird assembly points. The National Audubon Society for example organizes an annual Christmas bird count across North America.

Other addicts may wander along a country road or a riverside; they may visit a local pond or sand quarry, an open bush or a swamp. It all depends upon how keen you are and what birds you want to see. As good a method as any is to sit quietly, even in your garden, and let the birds come to you. It's not an expensive hobby, but because our eyes are not as keen as those of birds, some form of optical equipment is essential.

BINOCULARS

Monoculars, binoculars and telescopes are readily available and cost anywhere from about thirty to several hundred dollars. A monocular is usually a sort of prismatic telescope; its prisms shorten the inter-lens light path to obtain a shorter and handier instrument. Binoculars are by far the most popular of the three, and good quality models at a reasonable price are entirely adequate for the job. A binocular consists of two monoculars aligned side by side and having a common focusing device. Although 'binoculars' is now common and accepted usage, I prefer the technically correct term 'binocular' when referring to a single instrument. Field glasses are uncommon vintage binoculars, without prisms, and were used by vintage generals and others until the modern prismatic type superseded this old design.

Binoculars come in several sizes and shapes and are labelled according to the power of their magnification (the first number) and the objective lens diameter as measured in millimetres (the second number). A third factor, the exit pupil diameter, is found by dividing the objective lens diameter by the magnification power. All three are important to consider when you are selecting a binocular.

If the magnification power reads 8x, it means that the Evening Grosbeak at your feeder would appear eight times larger through the binocular than it would when seen with the naked eye. Usually, bird-watchers use a magnification between 7 and 10 power, but in open surroundings, such as when watching gulls or ducks on water, a higher magnification may be desirable. Bear in mind that a binocular with a higher magnification (10x and over), is more expensive and accentuates problems associated with increased weight and size. Any vibration or shaking will be amplified, which can prove particularly disturbing under windy conditions and make a target difficult to keep in sight when the binocular is hand-held. For many people, anything physically larger than 7×50 is just too heavy and clumsy.

The next number engraved on the binocular body is the objective lens diameter. Most have diameters between 30 and 45 millimetres; the higher the number, the brighter the image you'll see.

The exit pupil diameter, given earlier, tells you how well the binocular will perform under low light conditions. For instance, a binocular marked 7×35 has an exit pupil diameter of five millimetres. Higher numbers mean better performance in poor light.

The commonest combinations are the small 7×35 and the larger 7×50. Between these two is the fairly common 8×40 version, which I prefer because it is appreciably better than the 7×35 and far less bulky than the 7×50. An optical rule of thumb, however, indicates an exit pupil diameter of 5 to 7mm, as these values match the average range of eye pupil diameter. Bulk aside, 7×50 is undoubtedly a good combination, particularly if you spend most of your time birding in shady areas, or at dusk or dawn.

Once you've decided on the magnification and brightness you desire, consider how much territory you need to cover at one glance. The field of view represents the width of vision that a binocular will provide at 1000 yards. Generally speaking, the higher the magnification power, the lower the field of view will be.

You can see a larger area and get a slightly better resolution with some binoculars classed as "wide angle"; but apart from that, they offer no real advantage to most bird-watchers. They require more sophisticated design and manufacturing techniques, which tends to make them more expensive and heavier than models with smaller fields of vision.

I would recommend, however, that in making your choice, you be guided by the use to which you will put the binocular . Remember that a casual bird watcher will not need or want to invest in the same equipment as an ornithologist. Try different styles for yourself before buying. In addition, make sure there are no colour fringes in the lens, where the image you see is surrounded by a faint rainbow halo. Poor resolution, when fine details of the image are not clearly defined, and distortions at the edge of the field of view are also signs of an inferior product.

A used binocular can often be a good buy, but should be checked out beforehand. Look for the words 'coated lenses' close to the number designation, and make sure that the lenses are clear and not bloomed, scratched, cracked or loose. A well kept binocular will be complete with lens caps and carrying case. Check that no dents or scores are evident, and that both eye piece rings are present.

One side of the binocular will have an adjustable eyepiece with a scale marked +2 – 0 – –2. Adjust this in conjunction with the central focusing wheel so that both your eyes are in focus simultaneously. Both adjustments should be sluggish, but not unduly stiff to operate. There should be nothing loose on or in the binocular to cause a rattle.

Focus the binocular on a small, distant scene, say a chimney and part of a roof, and hold steady on this picture. Now use one eye at a time, switching back and forth from one to the other. If the picture remains exactly the same when viewed with either eye or both eyes, the optics may be considered to be okay. Any change in picture, left, right, up or down, from eye to eye, indicates misaligned prisms. A blow or a fall is the usual cause of this trouble, and unless you are a demon for punishment, the purchase of such a binocular would be inadvisable. Like a precision instrument, a binocular must be handled and stored with care. The case and straps should be checked periodically for wear as a sudden breakage can cause loss or damage.

EDITOR'S NOTE
According to Bruce Dilabio, a naturalist for The Canadian Nature Federation, when it comes to a focusing system for binoculars, you have only two choices — the traditional centre wheel or the Insta-Focus lever mechanism. The lever is faster, but you need to use both hands to focus accurately, and the mechanism tends to develop play over time. The traditional centre focussing wheel allows you to adjust the image with one hand, and fine-tune it more precisely than you can with the Insta-Focus system. Finally, you should consider prism design. They also come in two varieties; the standard, or Porro Prism system and the Roof Prism design. Although binoculars with the Roof Prism design are considerably more expensive, their performance is superior. Best of all, they have a particularly compact folded light path, which allows for a considerable reduction in bulk and weight.

BIRD SHELVES

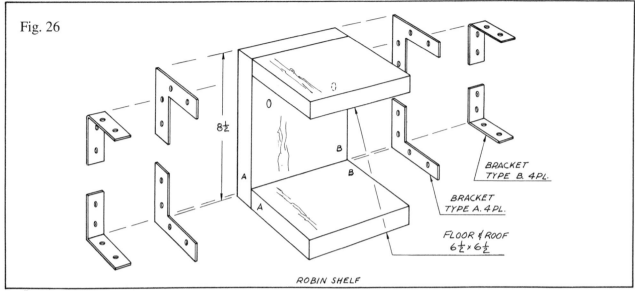

Fig. 26

$8\frac{1}{2}$

BRACKET
TYPE B. 4 PL.

BRACKET
TYPE A. 4 PL.

FLOOR & ROOF
$6\frac{1}{2} \times 6\frac{1}{2}$

ROBIN SHELF

The shelf shown in Fig. 26 requires very little explanation as it consists of only three pieces of wood. The shelf can be made by simply nailing the roof and floor to the back with six nails and ignoring all bracketry, in which case the grain of the roof and floor should be turned 90 degrees from that shown, to obtain a better grip for the nails. Without brackets, however, the joints are still weak; a much stronger assembly results from using four hardware store steel brackets of type A or B. These measure 3″×3″ to 4″×4″ and are screwed, or perhaps even nailed, to the surfaces marked A or B according to which type is used.

Two clearance holes are shown in the back for a pair of mounting screws or nails; alternatively, two keyholes could be used.

As the sides of the shelf are open, there is little point in rain slots or in sloping the roof, even though the type B brackets would allow a slight tilt-down at the front. To delay wood rot, the shelf should be brought in for winter.

Robins, Barn Swallows and Cliff Swallows seem to be the chief users of bird shelves, but a phoebe may also be a candidate. On occasion, a very few other birds have also been known to use shelves.

A robin shelf is larger than a swallow shelf, and is more likely to need a roof over it, as shown in Fig. 26, which shows only a floor (the shelf), a back and a roof.

Robins usually build their mud-lined grass nests in trees and bushes and prefer an open view around them. They are not cavity nesters and so are less inclined to use a shelf with sides on it. A roof is acceptable to them, however, probably because it hides the nest from above and provides partial protection from the weather. The shelf should be fastened to the wall of a shed, veranda or similar structure, preferably partially concealed by a creeper, a climbing rose, or other greenery.

As far as diet goes, robins score both good and bad. They eat cutworms, June bug larvae, caterpillars and similar pests, but they also eat a great many of the beneficial earthworms that keep our topsoil healthy. They are also accurate judges of the ripeness of small fruits, currants and the like, and relish them for dessert.

Robins seem to panic readily and are thought to be not too bright mentally, but they are not exactly dim either. Our few raspberry canes stand between two fence posts and were partially covered one summer with cheesecloth as 'protection'. I noticed a robin flitting from one post to the other, back and forth. Not wanting to tangle with the cheesecloth, he simply took such berries as he could see, one at a time and on the fly — no problem at all. Still, we have no reason to suppose that everything is arranged for our convenience, and it is nice to see a few robins prospecting around in the spring.

44

SWALLOW SHELVES

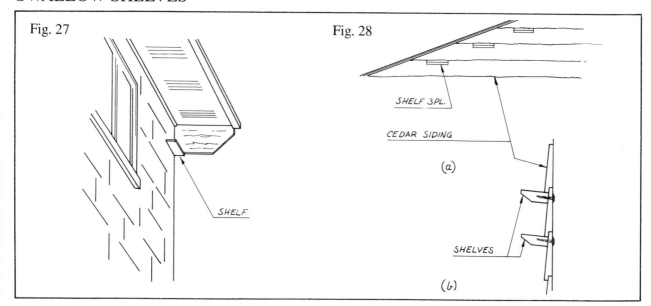

Fig. 27

Fig. 28

SHELF

SHELF 3 PL.

CEDAR SIDING

(a)

SHELVES

(b)

The shelf shown in Fig. 27 measures about 3½"×6" and is shown screwed to the lower edge of the plywood board at the end of a house. As the shelf in this position is unlikely to be knocked or disturbed, and the nest on it is small and weighs little, two screws are enough to hold it.

When we have access from within a veranda or shed, it allows us to use a neat shelf made from a 6" length of 2"×4". Its appearance would be clumsy without the chamfer (approx. 1"×2") on the lower front edge. Fig. 28(a) shows a front view of three such shelves mounted on cedar siding. Fig. 28(b) shows a side view and how the shelves rest against the edge of the clapboards and are secured with two screws apiece. Note that washers are used under the heads of the flat-head screws to prevent them from embedding deeply in the soft cedar.

As both Barn and Cliff Swallows are capable of bonding their mud nests surprisingly securely to a roughly surfaced vertical wall, even a small shelf will assist them appreciably. The nests may overhang and seem precarious, but their adhesive properties usually see them through the nesting season.

The shelf locations shown in Figs. 27 and 28 are typical, but swallows also like to nest under bridges, in culverts and other similar structures, often near water.

Barn Swallows, as the name implies, are given to nesting inside barns and sheds when allowed to do so. This usually means that a door has to be left open for them to reach their nests, which are often placed on a convenient beam or ledge, instead of being stuck to the side of the building as they would be outside.

As both types of swallow eat large numbers of flying insects all day long, a flock of either kind is very valuable to us in reducing pests such as mosquitoes and blackflies.

Eleven pairs of Cliff Swallows honoured us one year, some of which built their enclosed, spouted-hole mud nests on the shelves depicted in Fig. 28(a). Most built amicably, fetching their mud globs from the creek and packing them together. There was one Flash Harry type, however, who kept pinching his neighbour's newly laid globs, instead of fetching his own. He was told about it, and hammered many times, but it didn't seem to stop him (or her). His nest, however, was not completed until several days after those of his more industrious neighbours. It would appear that, like people, birds have individual characters, too.

CHAPTER 5.
BOXES FOR PURPLE MARTINS

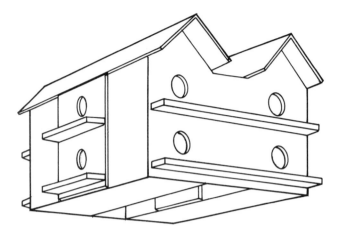

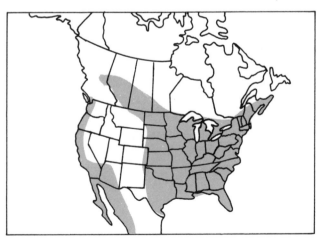

Most of the apartment houses for Purple Martins take a considerable amount of time and know-how, together with some cash, to bring into being. Before going ahead, it is therefore as well to know something about these large vigorous swallows and so become better able to estimate your chances of attracting them to your area. Admittedly, even empty, such a birdhouse enhances your garden, but a house with a colony of birds around it is a treasure that cannot be bought.

There has been considerable concern about the threats to migrating Purple Martins in recent years. The U.S. Fish and Wildlife Service is co-ordinating census efforts to determine the level of their overall numbers today. Strong male birds, known as 'scouts', often appear in spring ahead of the main flocks, but they will naturally return to where they nested previously before looking further afield for new housing. Even without an increase in the Purple Martin population, however, a house is still a worthwhile endeavour, as a few of those already in existence may rot and not be replaced; perhaps an owner dies, or moves away, and so dispossesses his colony. In this case your chances improve, particularly if you live nearby; it's a bit like going fishing, you never know your luck. Sometimes it takes several years to start a colony so it is best to just set up shop and hope.

As seen in Chapter 2, the relocation of colonies does not work, and so is not a feasible way of starting up in business, but there is another possibility. You make a tape recording of the birds' 'chip chop' voices, as heard at a successful colony, and then play it back, skywards, at home. The tape should be continuous; an old reel-to-reel recorder with a spliced loop will serve, repetition being unimportant. The recorder is placed inside your home and two wires are laid to an upside down cardboard carton placed outside near the Martin house. Two or three old radio loudspeakers, facing upwards through suitable holes cut in the bottom of the carton, send the calls into the sky. A calm day, clear and dry, is necessary, as rain would ruin the speakers. Birds have excellent hearing so do NOT try to simulate a fairground — it will just scare the birds away. Sound carries well on a still day and one or two watts R.M.S. of audio are entirely adequate.

Another reason for the low volume approach is that it

will upset other brands of swallow as little as possible. Tree Swallows, for example, tend to cruise around looking for the enemy and dive bombing the speaker cabinet. My long-term resident crew of ten to twenty Tree Swallows always teams up to repel boarders and claim their airspace. It is a simple case of incompatibility.

NEST SITE

Purple Martins prefer to have open space around their apartment house, with water or a somewhat swampy area not too far away, to provide food. House height varies from 7′ to 30′ or more. As few areas are free of flying pests like mosquitoes and black flies, the birds will nest in widely differing locales: on a busy marina jetty, a country or cottage environment, in small villages and towns, or in city suburbs. It is very significant that, wherever found, the Purple Martin colonies of today almost always utilize a man-made apartment house of some description; their once available nest sites are now almost non-existent — which is as good a reason as any for making another home for them.

TYPES OF INSTALLATION

Most Purple Martin apartment houses are set on poles of one sort or another, some fixed, some pivoting at the base. Despite being quite common, both these types generally require a ladder for inspection purposes.

Although an awkward rig, a pivoting pole does allow the box to be lowered, but as it also involves turning the house on its side, which would bring ruin to any eggs and young, it is only useful when the house is empty. In view of this, it seems best to use a fixed pole and to slide the house up and down it, a less common, but very convenient arrangement.

A Martin house can be hauled up its supporting pole by means of a rope and one or two pulleys, but this is not easy to do when a large and heavy house is involved. The problem can be solved by using a hollow pole with a counterweight sliding inside it, cables and pulleys completing the arrangement. Damp may be a problem inside the pole, and poor access to the concealed cable and its attachments can make inspection or servicing more difficult.

CAUTION: Being basically heavy objects on high poles, Martin houses, unless carefully handled, can be dangerous to all concerned. If a ladder is used against a pole, for example, either pole or ladder may break. A house on a pivoting pole can swing down too fast and hit someone. Similarly, on sliding houses, cables may break, and either the house or a counterweight can fall and hurt somebody. Frequent checks, good maintenance and careful handling are essential safety measures.

The Martin house under consideration has twelve nest boxes, which are quite enough for an initial investment. More houses can be made if required.

Basically, the house consists of two main sections of six nest boxes each. For installation, these are placed on opposite sides of a (nominally) 4″ square cedar pole and screwed together by means of two end covers. The whole house can then slide up and down the pole using cables and clothesline pulleys in conjunction with a pair of counterweights which pass between the two sections.

Weights not quite heavy enough to balance the house are easiest to use, along with plastic covered multi-strand flexible steel clothesline or boat cable. It is also possible to use ⅜″ nylon cables with smaller weights to keep them on their pulleys. The house is then hauled up by hand and the cables lashed around cleats at the base of the pole; this arrangement is, however, much less convenient and more difficult to operate. See photos 8-11 on pages 59 & 60 for the finished house. Photos 12-14 on page 61 show other designs of purple martin house which appeared in Lee Valley Tool's Great Canadian Bird House Contest. The heavier houses, such as that of photo 14, require the use of strong cables and a winch to raise them into position. Other houses from the competition appear on pages 63 & 64.

CONSTRUCTION

Where hot summers are the norm, it may be preferable to use weatherproof perforated ¼″ pegboard for the upper floor, taking into account a few small dimensional changes. Two or three ½″ holes in the covers, symmetrically placed on a line 5″ up from the floor holes, would also help. A few holes in the end boxes' lower floor can be added at any time but are not included in the figures.

Fig. 29 shows how the floors, walls and roofs can be cut from a single 4′×8′ sheet of 5/16″ exterior grade fir plywood; a cutting allowance of ⅛″ is shown by short lines on the appropriate side of a cut. Figs. 30 to 39 give

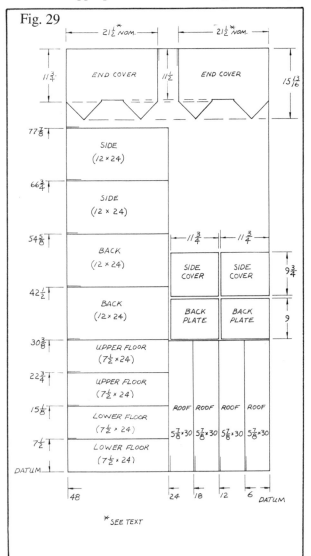

further details of the pieces, where applicable, and Figs. 40 and 41 show how they are put together.

The pieces in Fig. 29 are laid out to enable easy separation and minimum wood wastage. After marking out is completed, it is best to cut the sheet in half, lengthwise, and to follow on with the other cuts, observing the allowances as marked. Sand each piece smooth, especially the edges. Any splinters should be removed or glued back in place and clamped until firm again.

Cut out the entrance holes in the side and end covers, preferably using a hole saw in a slow-speed drill press. Safety calls for clamping the work to the drill press table on a piece of scrap plywood for each hole.

In two of the four roof sections, drill a ¼″ hole at 45 degrees on the centre line, 1¾″ from a long edge, for the hook shown in Fig. 39.

Holes ½″ or more in diameter may be drilled in the corners of the cutouts in Fig. 32, if desired, and joined up with a fret saw, or a sabre saw may be used to cut lines as drawn. Note that the four partitions of Fig. 34 are of ¾″ thick solid wood and not 5/16″ plywood. Also of solid wood are the shelves in Figs. 30 and 31 and the various glue blocks and battens of Figs. 35 to 37, 40 and 41.

Most Martin houses are painted white, and a dark waterproof stain on the six shelves makes a pleasant contrast. When desired, such staining should be done as soon as possible, the shelves only being nailed to their already painted covers on completion. This gives a sharp appearance without calling for masking or careful painting. The vertical batten, cedar shingles and the cedar pole should be treated likewise after work on them is completed.

END COVER LENGTH

When it is run up the pole, the house is held firmly in place by the interaction of two pairs of cedar shingles, one pair of which is shown in Fig. 41. The pole shingles lie thick end up and the house shingles lie thick end down, thus enabling them to mesh together. The thickness of the shingles, their degree of meshing, and the exact side measurement of the cedar pole govern the dimension x in Fig. 30. Varying x from 0 to +⅛″ or so, is the only way of obtaining an accurate end-cover length to suit your particular shingles and pole.

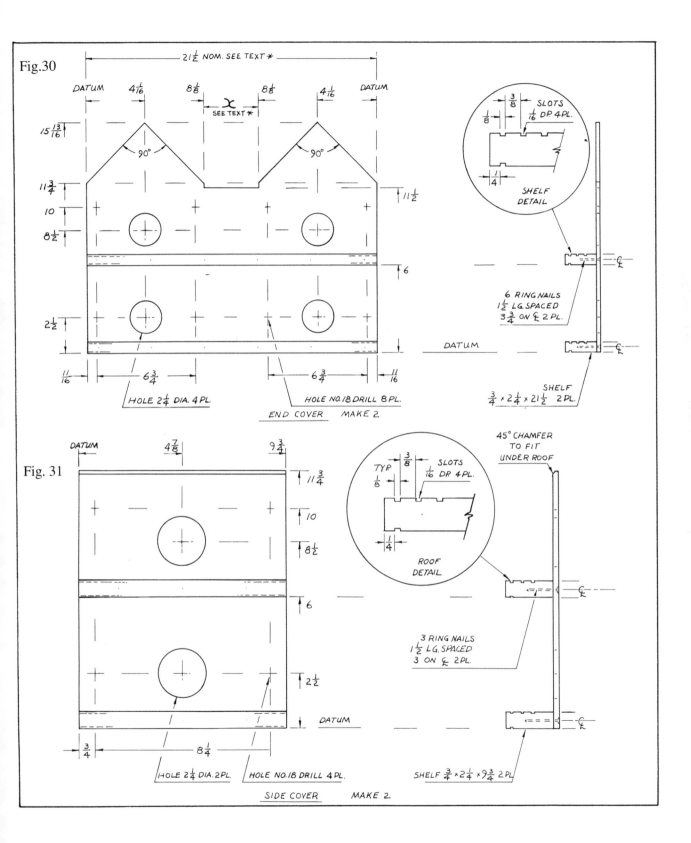

Fig.30

END COVER   MAKE 2

HOLE 2¼ DIA. 4 PL.

HOLE NO.18 DRILL 8 PL.

SHELF DETAIL

6 RING NAILS 1½ LG. SPACED 3¾ ON ₵ 2 PL.

SHELF ¾ × 2¼ × 21½ 2 PL.

Fig. 31

SIDE COVER   MAKE 2

HOLE 2¼ DIA. 2PL.

HOLE NO.18 DRILL 4 PL.

ROOF DETAIL

45° CHAMFER TO FIT UNDER ROOF

3 RING NAILS 1½ LG. SPACED 3 ON ₵ 2 PL.

SHELF ¾ × 2¼ × 9¾ 2 PL

49

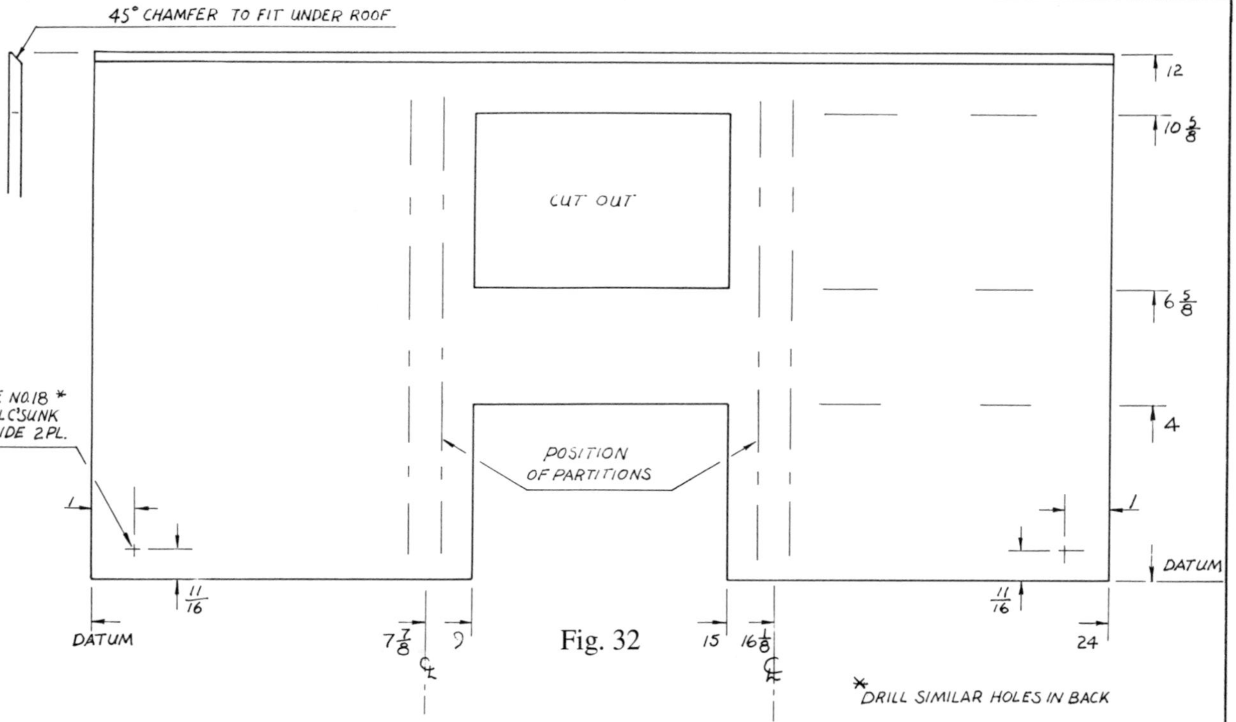
45° CHAMFER TO FIT UNDER ROOF
CUT OUT
HOLE NO.18 *
DRILL C'SUNK
TOPSIDE 2 PL.
POSITION
OF PARTITIONS
12
$10\frac{5}{8}$
$6\frac{5}{8}$
4
1
1
DATUM
$\frac{11}{16}$
$\frac{11}{16}$
DATUM
$7\frac{7}{8}$
9
15
$16\frac{1}{8}$
24
*DRILL SIMILAR HOLES IN BACK

Fig. 32

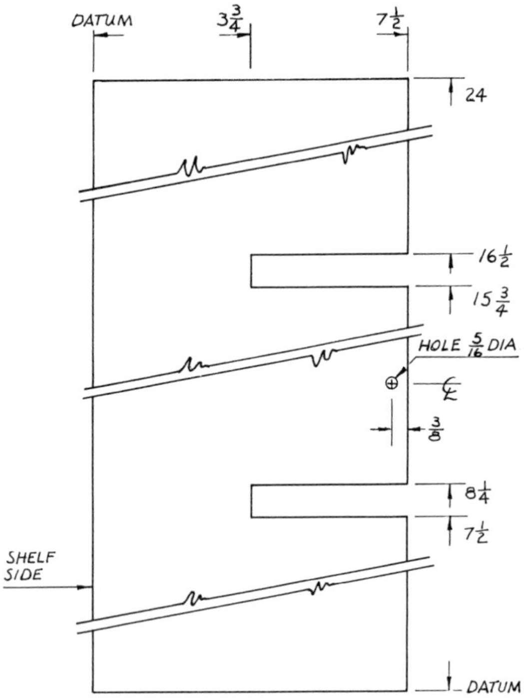
DATUM
$3\frac{3}{4}$
$7\frac{1}{2}$
24
$16\frac{1}{2}$
$15\frac{3}{4}$
HOLE $\frac{5}{16}$ DIA
$\frac{3}{8}$
$8\frac{1}{4}$
$7\frac{1}{2}$
SHELF
SIDE
DATUM

Fig. 33

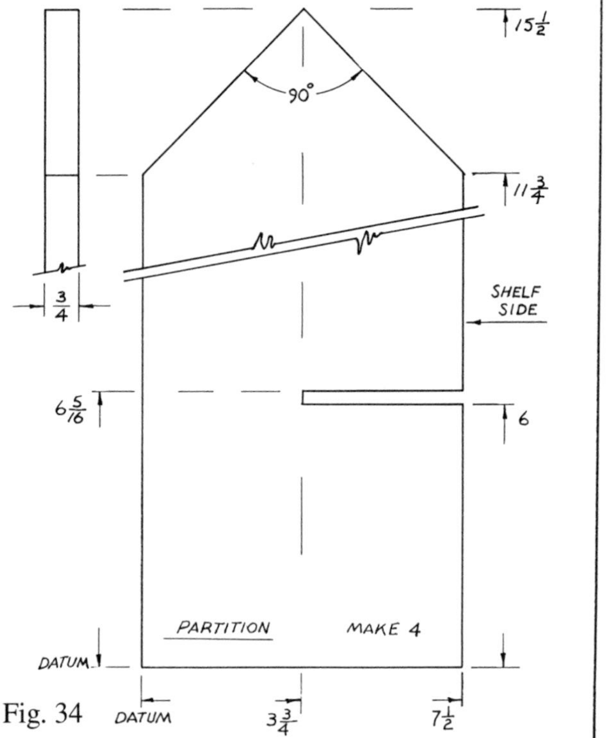
$15\frac{1}{2}$
90°
$11\frac{3}{4}$
$\frac{3}{4}$
SHELF
SIDE
$6\frac{5}{16}$
6
PARTITION
MAKE 4
DATUM
DATUM
$3\frac{3}{4}$
$7\frac{1}{2}$

Fig. 34

Cedar shingles generally taper from about $\frac{3}{8}''$ down to $\frac{1}{8}''$ which gives a mid-length thickness of $\frac{1}{4}''$, so four of them fully meshed, as on the pole, with their ends coincident, will total $4\times\frac{1}{4}'' =1''$ in thickness. A so-called 4×4 cedar pole really measures $3\frac{5}{8}''\times3\frac{5}{8}''$, or more likely $3\frac{1}{2}''\times3\frac{1}{2}''$. It is essential, therefore, to actually measure these items before cutting out the end cover. Finding value x was never exactly popular, and fortunately is presently unnecessary. Even so, it is because x may vary a trifle that the fixed dimensions of Fig. 30 are referenced from each end, instead of from the usual single Datum line; cutting out should be done accordingly.

In practice, the end-cover length is simply the sum of: (1) the average thickness of your four cedar shingles, plus (2) the actual side dimension of the cedar pole, plus (3) 17″. The figure of 17″ is made up of six $\frac{5}{16}''$ wall thicknesses and two $7\frac{1}{2}''$ floor side dimensions, plus $\frac{1}{8}''$ clearance, i.e. $1\frac{7}{8}'' + 15'' + \frac{1}{8}'' = 17''$. Adding typical shingle values of $4\times\frac{1}{4} = 1$ and a typical pole side dimension of $3\frac{1}{2}$ gives $17 + 1 + 3\frac{1}{2} = 21\frac{1}{2}$, as given in Fig. 30.

Cut out the $\frac{3}{4}''$ battens as shown in Figs. 35 and 36 and drill them as required. The $\frac{1}{4}''$ hole in the hook batten is critical, and must be carefully marked out and drilled squarely. From $\frac{3}{4}''$ thick wood, such as pine, cut the glue blocks as shown in Fig. 40 to the lengths shown in Table 2.

Glue Block	Length(in.)	No. Req'd	Data
GB1	$2\frac{1}{2}$ to 3	4	
GB2	$2\frac{1}{2}$	4	one end bevelled at 45° as shown
GB3	$1\frac{1}{2}$	12	triangular section
GB4	$6\frac{3}{4}$ nom.	8	bevel one end at 45° as shown and trim to suit when fitted
GB5	$5\frac{3}{4}$+ see data	8	length added to height of GB6 to equal 6″
GB 6	4	8	

The $\frac{1}{4}''$ radio shaft coupler shown in Fig. 38 may be a discontinued item for electronics suppliers, but can be reproduced on a lathe quite simply. Alternatively, two separate collars from an engineering supply house may be substituted. Components of this kind usually come with slot-head or Allen set screws. The slot type often breaks off, and if limited access makes the Allen type awkward to tighten, it is best to replace them with $\frac{3}{32}''$ or $\frac{1}{4}''$ stainless steel screws. Note that a cheap steel #6-32 screw is also likely to break off as this particular size has a relatively weak core, #8-32 being much stronger.

The hook of Fig. 39 is made by bending the end of a 14″ length of $\frac{1}{4}''$ dia. cold rolled mild steel rod around a $\frac{3}{4}''$ rod in the vise and removing all burrs. The $\frac{1}{2}''\times\frac{1}{32}''$ flat on the other end is important for safety reasons and <u>must not be omitted</u>. It is easily filed into the shaft.

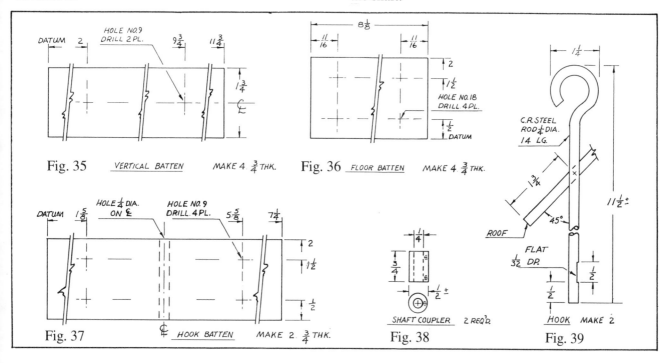

Fig. 35   VERTICAL BATTEN   MAKE 4 $\frac{3}{4}$ THK.   Fig. 36   FLOOR BATTEN   MAKE 4 $\frac{3}{4}$ THK.

Fig. 37   HOOK BATTEN   MAKE 2 $\frac{3}{4}$ THK.

SHAFT COUPLER   2 REQ'D   Fig. 38

HOOK   MAKE 2   Fig. 39

ASSEMBLY

In the interests of clarity, the assembly of only one of the two sections is described below, the other being identical.

Chamfer the top edge of the back to fit under the roof overhang, using a partition and Fig. 41 as a guide. Mark the centre of the top and bottom edges of the back and back-plate, and glue and clamp them together with their lower edges and centre marks aligned.

On the inside of the back, mark out a line parallel to the bottom edge and exactly $6\frac{5}{16}''$ from it. This line indicates the underside of the upper floor. Measuring from each end, mark out the exact centre point of the line. Glue and clamp the hook batten in place with its upper edge on the line and the centre of the $\frac{1}{4}''$ hole aligned accurately with the centre point of the line. Check that the batten did not shift when clamped, and adjust it as required. Accuracy is required here to avoid later problems.

When the glue is set, extend the four holes in the batten through both back and back-plate with a no. 9 drill, and bolt the three pieces together with four $2''$, 10–32 steel screws, eight washers (about $\frac{1}{2}''$ OD), and four lock nuts, as shown in Fig. 41. If a no. 9 drill is not available, a $\frac{3}{16}''$ drill will give a tighter but workable fit.

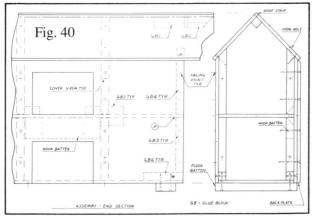

Fig. 40

On the lower floor, mark out a partition check line $7\frac{1}{2}''$ from each end and a partition centre line at $7\frac{7}{8}''$. On the centre line drill two $\frac{1}{16}''$ holes about $1\frac{1}{2}''$ from each edge. Align the partitions to the check lines and using $2''$ ring nails, partially nail the lower floor to the partitions and slide the interlocking top floor into place. Check that the partitions have not shifted from the check lines and are still sensibly parallel. If need be, trim the slots so that the partitions, and both floors, are respectively parallel to each other. This achieved, complete the nailing.

Using a method similar to that above, mark out partition lines on two roof sections, the partition check line being at $10\frac{1}{2}''$ and the centre line $10\frac{7}{8}''$ from each end. Noting that there is NO OVERLAP at the peak (Fig. 40) set the roof sections accurately on the partitions and nail them in place. Chamfer the top edge of the side, as necessary, (Fig. 32) and nail the SIDE to the partitions on their SHELF SIDE (Fig. 34); a good nailing pattern is shown, dotted, in Fig. 40. This orientation presents the unslotted sides of the partitions to the back and results in a slightly stronger assembly.

Check that the back fits correctly, level with the lower floor, and adjust the top edge chamfer, if necessary, so that it fits under the roof overhang, (Fig. 41). Mark out two lines on the back corresponding to the centre lines

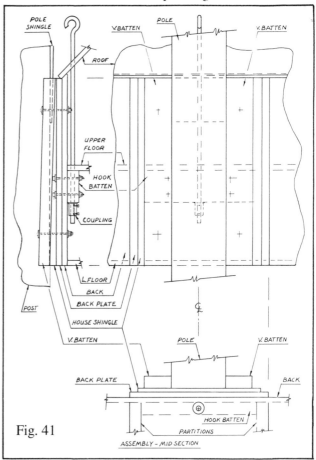

Fig. 41

of the partitions (they will be $7\frac{7}{8}''$ from each end) and drill four holes, with a no. 9 drill, on each line to the same pattern as the side retaining nails, (ringed dots), shown in Fig. 40. Countersink these eight holes in the back-plate to accept $2''$ no. 10 F.H. (flat-head) steel screws. Fit the back on correctly and partially screw it in place. Verify that a $\frac{1}{4}''$ rod or bolt will pass through the upper floor and the hook batten, and then drive the screws down fully. A no. 10 screw does not usually split $\frac{3}{4}''$ pine, but if the partitions are of say, fir, predrilling with a $\frac{7}{64}''$ or no. 36 drill is advisable.

Glue and clamp a floor batten, squarely centred, in place (Fig. 40), resting a GB5 (glue block no. 5) along-side it to space it $\frac{3}{4}''$ from the end of the floor. Extend the four no. 18 drill holes through the floor and glue and screw two GB6's in place with $2''$ no. 8 F.H. steel screws. Glue the side of the GB6's and screw two $1''$ no. 8 F.H. steel screws into them through the holes in the side and the back.

Set two GB5's in place (Fig. 40) and cut a piece of scrap wood about $4''$ wide and $\frac{3}{4}''$ or more thick so that it fits exactly between them. The spacer thus made will be close to $6''$ in length.

Remove the spacer and adjust the lengths of the GB5's so that when in position, they ensure that there is exactly $6''$ between the two floors. Glue the two GB5's in position, flush with the ends, and with the spacer between them. Glue blocks only stay in place when individually fitted. Both surfaces have to contact fully and must be trimmed to suit if any teetering is evident. Set the section down FLAT on the bench with the roof clear, and drive two $1''$ ring nails through the back into the GB5 and two more likewise through the side. The nailing pattern is shown by the dots in Fig. 40. Remove the space and clamp both sides, as required, to ensure sound glue joints.

Repeat the above procedure at the other end of the section. Cut the square ends of the GB4's so that they fit snugly when the roof, side and back are all in correct juxtaposition. Use the same spacer and the method given above to glue and nail them in place. The four corner screws in the roof are $1\frac{1}{4}''$ no. 8 F.H. size, and should be put in last when all else is secure.

Mark out and drill the 45 degree $\frac{1}{4}''$ dia. hook hole

$1\frac{3}{4}''$ in from the exact centre of the roof edge which lies above the back-plate, see Fig. 39. Verify that the hook will pass through the roof, upper floor and hook batten. A firm fit is desirable.

Cut a cedar shingle $11\frac{3}{4}''$ long × $8''$ wide, and mark out its lengthwise centre line. Lay the shingle, thin end up, on the back-plate with its centre line and its top and bottom aligned with those of the back-plate. Apply a firm pressure on the shingle over the 10–32 hook batten screw heads so as to impress them slightly into the cedar. Drill $\frac{1}{2}''$ clearance holes at these points so that the shingle can lie flat against the back-plate in the desired position. Hammer in two or three small nails, close to the long edges to secure it on a temporary basis, see Fig. 41.

The house will be amply high enough on a cedar pole 14' long. Taking the previous side dimension of $3\frac{1}{2}''$ and $\frac{1}{8}''$ for clearance gives us $3\frac{5}{8}''$. Draw two lines parallel to the shingle centre line and spaced half this distance from it, $3\frac{5}{8}'' \div 2 = 1\frac{13}{16}''$. Lay two battens on the shingle, aligned top and bottom with it, and with one edge on each line as shown in Fig. 41. Hold these firmly in position and drill through the battens, shingle, back-plate and back, with a no. 9 drill. Screw these four items together firmly with four $2\frac{1}{4}''$, 10-32 steel screws, eight washers (about $\frac{1}{2}''$ O.D.), and four lock nuts. Check that the pole will slide easily between the battens at 90 degrees to the bottom of the house section.

Close any small wall-to-floor gaps with thin $1''$ ring nails as at point P in Fig 40, taking care to centralize the nails in the edge of the $\frac{5}{16}''$ plywood and so avoid splitting.

Fit the remaining glue blocks GB1, 2 and 3 as given in Fig. 40. GB1 and GB2 are spaced $\frac{5}{16}''$ apart to accept and steady the tip of the end cover. This slot must, of course, line up with the end of the house section.

Cut a $\frac{5}{16}''$ square strip of pine $30''$ long and glue it in place along the peak of the roof. Strips of masking tape pulled tight across it are enough to hold it until the glue sets. The top edge should then be sanded slightly round.

Fit the hook in place and tighten up the two screws in its coupling or collars. After completing the second section of the house, fill the clearance holes in the shingles with a good sealer and seal around the hook-roof gap and along the roof peak. Check that the side covers fit and adjust their top edge chamfers as required. Set the end covers carefully in place and screw them on with sixteen 1″ no. 8 round-head brass screws. Check that the pole has adequate clearance. Fit the side covers likewise and then remove all four covers.

Although a stained Martin house is feasible, a white house is cooler for the birds. Give the complete house a final sanding and check, and then apply a coat of latex primer followed by two coats of exterior white latex paint to both the inside and outside surfaces. Leaded paints are not to be used as their flakes poison the young birds when they nibble them.

When the paint is thoroughly dry and the house is to be installed, fit the two side covers on again, leaving the end covers off.

THE POLE

Each of the two pulleys must allow its cable to run squarely down the centre line of one side of the 14′ long pole. The arrangement of Fig. 42 gives the cables a good alignment along the sides of the pole.

Mark out two lines around the pole, at 3″ and 9″ from the top, and use them as a basis for chiselling out the two bevels shown in Fig. 42. The bevels are 6″ long and 2″ wide and are indented 1″ from each corner, their ends being angled at approximately 45 degrees. Mark out the centre of each bevel 6″ down from the top of the pole, and drill a ¼″ dia. guide hole from each side to meet in the middle.

Two 5″ clothesline pulleys and a steel shaft on which they turn smoothly without undue play are required. Drill the two cotter pin holes in the shaft. Their distance apart

will be the bevel-to-bevel distance (in our case a little less that 3″) plus two pulley thicknesses, plus four washer thicknesses (4″×¹⁄₁₆″ = ¼″) plus ⅛″ for clearance. (A ⅜″ shaft some 6½″ long is typical.) Drill out the hole in the pole slightly undersize, so that the shaft is held firmly when tapped in with a block of wood and a hammer.

Cut two cedar shingles to the same width as the pole and glue and nail them to opposite sides of the pole with 1″ and 1½″ ring nails. The thick ends of the shingles are uppermost and are 18″ from the top of the pole. Tap the nail heads down well so that none project to score the house shingles.

A pointed pole looks well, but an array of perches is even more to the point as far as birds are concerned, and will be used continually in preference to the house roof which offers them less purchase. The array pictured in photos nos. 8, 10 and 11 on pages 59 & 60 also protects the pole end-grain from the weather.

These perches are very simple to make. Cut four lengths of ¾″ square pine or fir about 24″ long and round them for a distance of 8″ from each end with a spokeshave or coarse file. Cut a 7″×7″ square of ¾″ exterior grade plywood, and nail a perch, with equal overhangs, to each of two opposite edges of the square. Nail the other two perches symmetrically to the top of the square, close to the edges, at 90 degrees to the first pair. See photo 8, page 59 for the completed array.

Apply two liberal coats of stain to the lower 4′ of the pole. When all is dry again, fit the washers, pulleys and cotter pins and adjust the shaft, as required for equal play both sides. Nail the array to the top of the pole with four 3″ spiral nails.

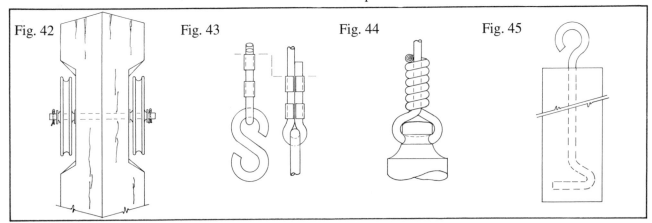

Fig. 42   Fig. 43   Fig. 44   Fig. 45

THE WEIGHTS

The complete house weighs almost 35 lb. so two 16 lb. counterweights will almost balance it. Table 3 shows three typical configurations with dimensions rounded to the nearest ½".

Metal	Dia.(in.)	Length(in.)	Weight (lbs.)
Steel @ 0.28 lbs./cu."	2¼	14½	16
Steel @ 0.28 lbs./cu."	2⅜	13	16
Lead @ 0.41 lbs./cu."	2	12.5	16

A typical hot-rolled steel sash-weight is shown in Fig. 44. Note that at least six turns of plastic-covered clothesline are necessary for this type of cable fastening to be secure. Boat cable is too springy and flexible for this method and requires screwed cleats. The usual steel cleats supplied with clothesline, Fig. 43, are also good, but need to be checked regularly as they have a tendency to release and slide. Always use at least two per fastening, as shown in the clothesline hook, Fig. 43, which engages with the Martin house hook.

Although steel is cheaper than lead, it is somewhat harder to deal with. One way is to use an available small sash weight and jam or pin it into a suitable steel pipe to make up the requisite poundage. Grandfather clock weights at 13 or 14 lb. are not recommended for this application as their hook attachment is sometimes in doubt.

If steel is not readily available, it is not difficult to make a hook of ¼" steel rod and cast a lead weight in a piece of steel pipe, along the lines shown in Fig. 45. The formula for the volume of a cylinder is:

$$V = \pi r^2 l$$

Where V = the volume in cubic inches
π = 3.14
r = the radius of the cylinder in inches.
l = the length of the cylinder in inches.

Lead-pouring ceremonies, where feasible, are perhaps best done in the fall when a small brush pile has accumulated to provide the necessary heat.

INSTALLATION

At an open site, as described earlier, dig a hole at least 3′ deep, keeping it as narrow as possible. Set the pole in place and turn it, as desired. Fill the hole in, tamping the earth every few inches as it rises around the pole and using a spirit level to keep it vertical.

As the pulleys are now about 10′ 6″ up, each of the two cables will be close to 10′ 6″ long, assuming a 14″ weight with 3″ of space under it when the house is fully up. This should be verified practically, to allow for any discrepancies in pulley height and weight length. Fasten a cleated hook, Fig. 43, to the free end of a coil of new plastic-covered steel clothesline cable, and hook it to one of the house sections. Hauling it up the pole to its correct level will enable the cable length to be ascertained. It is wise to leave the cables initially overlength.

Note that a termination with cleats, as in Fig 43, requires 3″ of extra cable, and a wrap-around of 6+ turns as in Fig. 44, requires at least 12″. Unless the sash-weight loop of Fig. 44 is used, it is a good idea to cleat substantial 'S' hooks to both ends of each cable. For the figures given above, an off-the-coil length of some 13′ is typically sufficient.

Two auxiliary cables of similar but less critical length are required, each having a cleated hook at one end. These hook onto the free ends of the weight cables and so facilitate raising and lowering the weights.

By means of the auxiliary cables, raise the weights, one at a time, until the house sections can be hooked on as shown in photo no. 9 on page 59. A house section with end cover weighs about 1½ lb. less than the weight, and so will tend to rise, so it is as well to have a friend steady the sections against the pole while the end covers are being screwed on. The house can then be run up GENTLY, repeat GENTLY, until the shingles mesh. The operation is very smooth and easy, so there is always a tendency to go fast, thus jamming the house and even straining it; a stepladder may be needed to free it again.

With the house in position, the cable length can be finalized and the auxiliary cables used to lash the weights to the foot of the pole. When the house is to be taken down, slapping the full length of the weights GENTLY against the pole should be enough to free the house and start its descent.

The auxiliary cables then replace the house sections and allow the weights to be lowered onto two building blocks and lashed in place again for winter. If the weights were lowered to ground level, their cable would come off the pulleys. The blocks are simply rotated 90 degrees around the pole for summer use and the weights fall between them. The blocks also protect the weights and pole from accidental damage from say, a lawnmower. Photos 9 to 11 show how the house is installed.

The installation is very convenient and easy to use and the weights are lashed down most of the time, but always stand from under when raising or lowering the house.

Once the house is installed in spring, it is important to keep pests from taking over, even if Purple Martins fail to appear. It is not necessary to take the covers off to remove unwanted nesting material; it can simply be hooked out through the entrance hole with a bent piece of coathanger wire.

A longtime Purple Martin fancier once told me of how he got his annual production of young Martins as high as 56, chiefly by controlling starlings and House Sparrows. Other activities then intervened, his pest elimination programme lapsed for a while - and production dropped to 21. He then went back to using his sliding shutter rig whenever a pest entered a nest box, and he thus eliminated 29 of the enemy. His score of young Martins then rose to 34. These statistics, it seems, took five years of record keeping to obtain, but they do show how aggressive, imported species can affect our native birds.

The same dedicated 'martineer' once saved his newly returned flock from a killing late frost. The entire contingent had crammed itself into one box to keep warm. He managed to remove the huddled mass of birds and take them indoors to thaw out. Finely chopped hamburger kept them ticking over until better weather returned, and all survived.

Photos No. 12 to 14 on page 61 show three other Purple Martin house designs. No. 12 shows an 18 box house by Don Bird of Truro, N.S. It is made of $7/16"$ poplar plywood and the weight is given as about 28 lb. The entrance holes are $2\frac{1}{4}"$ in dia. and central ventilation is provided around the $1\frac{1}{2}$ nom. dia. central pipe which supports the house.

Photo no. 13 shows a 32 box design by Jim McGuire of Kanata, Ont. Weighing about 60 lb., it is made of aluminum siding and mounts on a telescoping three section pole.

Photo no. 14 shows a kingsize, 54 box heavyweight by Jacques Lagueux of St. Germain, Que. Construction is of $\frac{1}{2}"$ Russian birch plywood joined together with 2-part weather-proof glue. Entrance hole size is $2\frac{1}{2}"$ and the house is winched up on a steel cable.

It is evident from this chapter that even a relatively small Purple Martin house entails a considerable amount of thought and careful effort to create. There is also some expense involved, and the project is somewhat of a gamble. The world's Purple Martins, however, are also gambling — with their lives — that you and I will build them a house to nest in, and so help them to survive.

Photo 4   *Winter Storage*

Photo 5   *A box with a bark roof and spring held lower front - note the covered springs*

Photo 6   *A box similar to that of section 2, page 18, but with a spring held lower front and sized for a Flicker*

Photo 7   *The Photo 6 box with the lower front open*

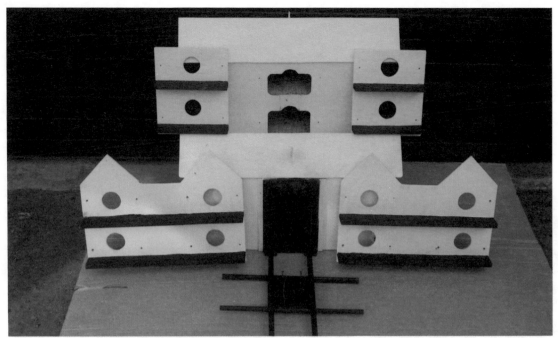

Photo 8   *Purple Martin House components*

Photo 9   *Purple Martin house installation*

Photo 10   *The Purple Martin house assembled around its pole and ready to raise*

Photo 11   *The Purple Martin House ready for business -note the lashed weights between their blocks*

Photo 12

Photo 14

Photo 13

Photo 12   *An 18 box Purple Martin house by Don Bird of Nova Scotia*

Photo 13   *A 32 box Purple Martin house by Jim McGuire of Kanata, Ontario*

Photo 14   *A 54 box Purple Martin house by Jacques Lagueux of St. Germain, Quebec*

Photo 15   *A tray feeder on a veranda sill*

Photo 16   *Underside of Fig. 15 feeder showing holding blocks and turnbuckles*

Photo 17   *A row of spray millet*

Photo 18   *Spray Millet - 12 inches long*

Photo 19   While the only limit to your birdhouse designs is your imagination, the preferences of your intended tenants should come first. The dowel-tips on the front of the house at top left are a good alternative to a perch beneath the hole, which should never be used.

Photo 20   *This house by Mr. H.G. Graves, of Ottawa,
was the winner in the Purple Martin class of The Great
Canadian Birdhouse Contest, sponsored by Lee Valley
Tools.*

CHAPTER 6.
BIRDFEEDERS, BIRDFOOD AND BIRDBATHS

Seed dispensing birdfeeders fall into two main categories; the hopper type, of Fig 46, and some form of open tray, as in Fig. 56. Hoppers work best with large seeds like those of the sunflower, which tend to slide easily. It is very difficult to keep windblown snow, and therefore water, out of a hopper. This makes them clog, and the bird food solidify, when hoppers are loaded with cracked corn and small seed mixes which are much more suited to a shallow tray.

When made entirely of plastic, hanging cylindrical hoppers are worth consideration. These have multiple feeding holes on several levels which allow several birds to eat at once, with fair shares for all. In some models, however, the feeding holes are formed from substantial metal castings screwed together; these are best avoided because of the danger of cold metal adhesions, both avian and human.

It is, of course, much more satisfying to make what you want, rather than to buy it, and the following hopper and tray add up to a very good feeding station.

A HOPPER FEEDER

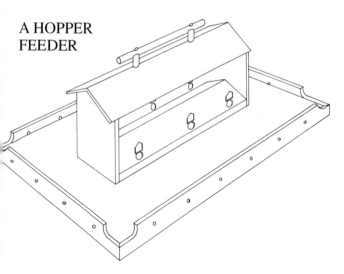

The hopper feeder of Figs. 46 to 54 is based on an excellent design by Leonard Lee. The spacious tray, (Figs. 53 and 54) permits a little mixed seed to be spread at the ends of the hopper, a versatile arrangement. The tray is surrounded by trim which provides a ¾″ high wall to stop the wind from blowing the seeds and husks away. All detritus, together with snow, can be scraped along the tray and pushed through a 4″ gap in the trim, as shown in the bottom right-hand corner of the tray in Fig. 53. The scraper of Fig. 55 is excellent for this purpose, and when it is not in use, it is handy for blocking the 4″ gap in the trim, as shown in Fig. 53. As it cannot be laid flush with the tray, it will not easily freeze to it. The scraper is simply a blade of arborite, fibreglass or printed circuit board epoxied into a slot in a wooden handle.

The 1″ feeding holes are far enough apart to enable simultaneous use without invoking the pecking order syndrome. Also, as the hopper is double sided, a Blue Jay on one side cannot see chickadees on the other side, and both species can eat together for a change. Experience shows that, without a restricting shelf, excessively fast seed flow at the 1″ holes causes wastage. The seed deflectors of Fig. 51 are designed to hold this undue outpouring in check. Further restriction can be achieved by gluing ⅛″ thick wood strips to the deflector sides and extending them to shield the sides of the feeding holes as well.

The roof of the hopper lifts off readily by means of its handle, Fig. 52, which also serves as a perch. The floor, Fig. 50, is sloped roof-fashion to channel the seeds towards the feeding holes. Its thickness enables secure mounting and also keeps the seed dry by raising it above the level of the tray.

When made to the dimensions given, the hopper volume is over half a cubic foot. Whilst it is not desirable to change the length of the hopper or the feeding hole layout, changes in volume are easily made by selecting other heights and widths prior to construction. For example, using a height of 14″ and increasing the width to 10″ will raise the volume to about one cubic foot; a tray measuring about 22″ × 28″ would then be required. Scaling down can be accomplished likewise, and a smaller tray could feasibly be supported by an 8″×8″×1¾″ pine offcut with a pipe flange bolted to it, as an alternative to the arrangement of Fig. 54.

CONSTRUCTION

The assembly drawing of the hopper is shown in Fig. 46, and Figs. 47 to 55 show the piece parts and tray. The whole feeder is made entirely of wood except for the sides of the hopper which are of ¼" clear plastic. This comes under several names such as Perspex, Lucite, Plexiglass and Acrylic. One of its many uses is to provide a sort of micro-rink on which up and coming young executives can roll their office chairs. Due to overactivity, or underactivity, these plastic sheets fracture from time to time and the cracked ones (not the executives) can be obtained fairly cheaply from the furniture dealers who supply replacements. Although a few surface abrasions and slight warps may be evident, they are not functionally significant and your customers are unlikely to complain.

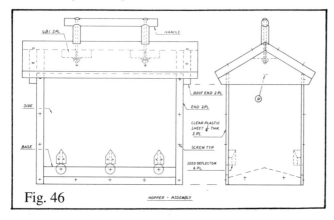

Fig. 46   HOPPER - ASSEMBLY

Choose as flat a piece of sheet as possible and cut out the sides shown in Fig. 47. This can be done accurately on the table saw, using a slow cut with a carbide tipped blade set low to avoid chipping. Mark out and drill all the holes. All seventeen screw holes should be counter-

sunk, the six seed deflector holes for ¾" or ⅞" no. 4 F.H. screws and the other eleven for 1" no. 8 F.H. screws. Flat-head screws are used to give sheer sides that have no projections to foul the scraper as it passes when cleaning up the tray.

The hopper ends of Fig. 48 can be made of solid wood such as pine or of marine or exterior grade plywood. The two holes indicated are for 2" no. 10 F.H. screws which secure the ends to the floor of Fig. 50. The roof ends of Fig. 49 are best made of solid pine or similar wood.

The floor of Fig. 50 is made from an offcut of 8" × 2" pine or two thinner pieces glued together if a higher ridge is considered desirable. For durability the seed deflectors are probably best made of oak, their screw holes being pre-drilled as shown in Fig. 47. When all screws seat properly, apply epoxy glue before final assembly; this will keep moisture out of the joint and thus enhance appearance.

The handle of Fig. 52 can also be of oak as it weathers better than say, birch. It is secured to the roof with two ¼" - 20 bolts 4½" long which pass through two ¾" × 3" long glue blocks to be held by two washers and lock nuts. These can be tightened should the handle loosen due to wood shrinkage. A plastic drawer handle is not really a viable substitute as its gap is usually too small to accept gloved fingers comfortably. In regions with cold winters, metal handles must not be used for the same reason as was given earlier regarding metal fittings — cold metal adhesions.

If you desire to hang the feeder, the handle can be exchanged for either one or two plastic-coated steel hooks. The roof must then be held on by means of two tapering ⅜" dia. oak dowels at point P of Figs. 46 and 49. To replenish the hanging version, it is necessary to unhook it and set it down before removing the tapered dowels and the roof.

No drawing is given for the roof, as it simply consists of two boards, each ¾"×6"×18", which are bevelled lengthwise at 60 degrees and glued firmly together when nailed to the roof ends shown in Figs. 46 and 49.

Fig. 53 shows a top view of the hopper and its tray with scaled-up side views of the trim and the 4" corner gap. Cut the 20"×28" tray from ¾" thick marine or exterior grade plywood. Make the four 21½" and 29½"

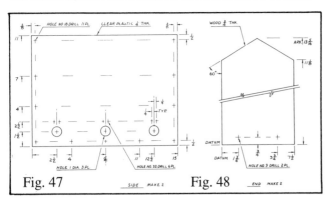

Fig. 47   SIDE   MAKE 2   Fig. 48   END   MAKE 2

Fig. 49

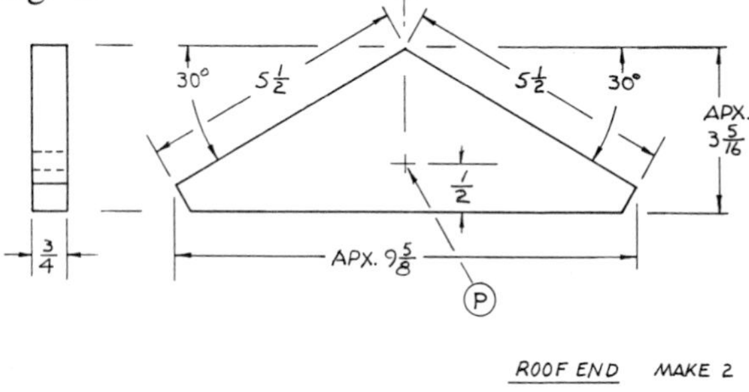
ROOF END MAKE 2

Fig.50

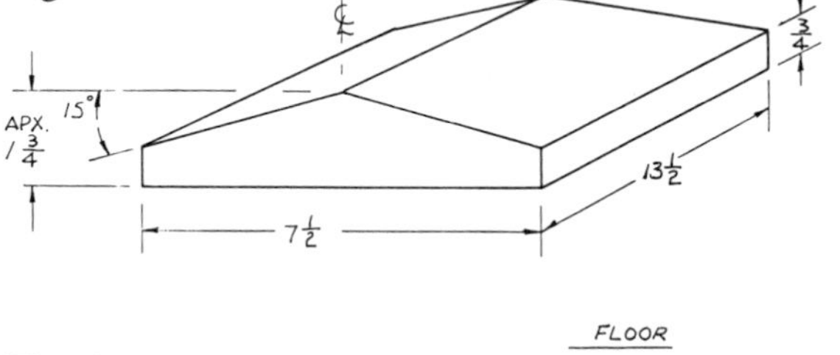
FLOOR

Fig. 51

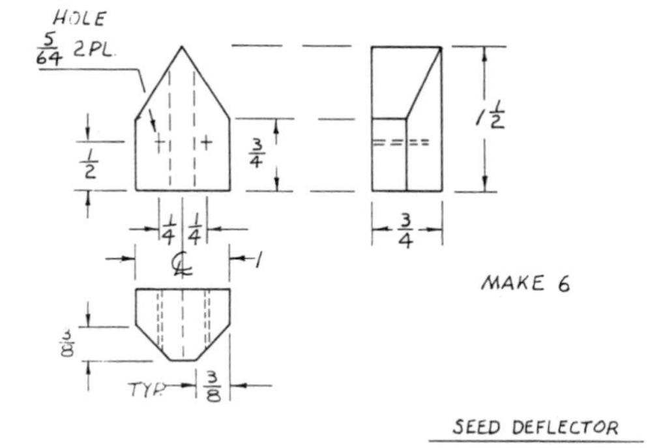
HOLE
MAKE 6
SEED DEFLECTOR

Fig. 52

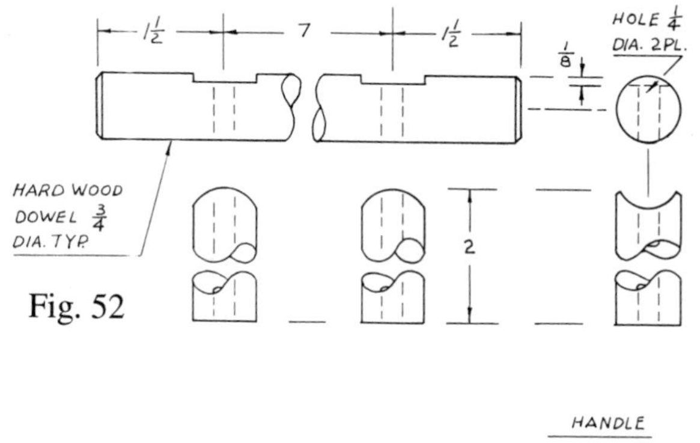
HOLE
HARD WOOD
DOWEL
HANDLE

Fig. 53

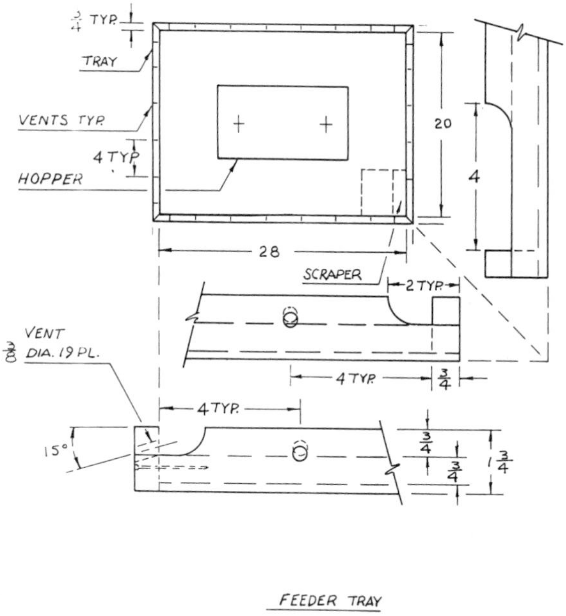
TRAY
VENTS TYP.
HOPPER
SCRAPER
VENT
FEEDER TRAY

long trim pieces from ¾″ thick pine and mitre their ends at 45 degrees. Half-inch oak trim is a better but more expensive alternative.

To prevent flooding, a gap is left at each corner and 10 sloping vent holes are drilled in the trim as shown in Fig. 53. Some of these vent holes may freeze and plug up from time to time, and although numerous, they are generally not as effective as small gaps in the trim.

The two screw hole locations marked '+' in the hopper outline of Fig. 53 are each 5″ from the centre of the long centre line. They denote two 5⁄16″×2″ lag bolts, with washers. The lag bolts pass upwards through the tray into the floor of the hopper to secure it. Mark out and drill these two holes in the tray.

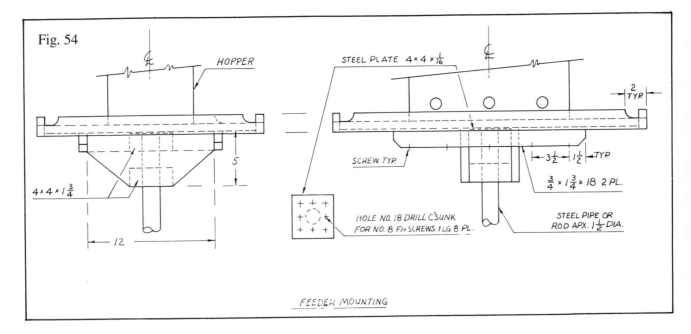

Fig. 54

HOPPER

STEEL PLATE 4×4×$\frac{1}{16}$

SCREW TYP.

HOLE NO. 18 DRILL C'SUNK
FOR NO. 8 F.H. SCREWS 1 LG 8 PL.

4×4×1$\frac{3}{4}$

5

12

2 TYP.

3$\frac{1}{2}$ | 1$\frac{1}{2}$ | TYP.

$\frac{3}{4}$ × 1$\frac{3}{4}$ × 18 2 PL.

STEEL PIPE OR
ROD APX. 1$\frac{1}{2}$ DIA.

FEEDER MOUNTING

Fig. 54 shows how the hopper and its tray can be mounted on a steel support of dia. 'D', say 1¼ to 1½". The support may be solid or hollow, fixed or movable. If total weight and size are considered, it is best to drive or dig the support into the ground so that a high wind will not blow the feeder over.

A tray height of four feet is probably a good compromise between operational convenience and predator inconvenience. If snow builds up in your area during the winter, a height-adjustable tray is a good idea. This is quite simple to incorporate by using a pipe sliding over a smaller pipe or solid rod. Holes 2" or 3" apart and ¼" in diameter are drilled in the pipe. A ¼" bolt and nut through the appropriate pair of holes then supports the end of the solid rod to hold the feeder at the desired height.

An even simpler way is to clamp a few inches of channel, such as a steel bed rail, to the rod with a couple of gear clamps. Whichever method is used, the rod should go in the ground and the pipe into the feeder, otherwise the pipe could fill with ice and so seize up the rod.

A fixed support will need to go down 20" to 30" into the ground and project some 48" above it, and so must be 6 to 6½" feet long. A three-foot pipe on a 6½ foot rod would be typical for the adjustable arrangement. Assembly is easy, as the pipe can be withdrawn from the tray.

Once the diameter 'D' has been determined, cut out the two 1¾"×4" blocks and on their exact centres cut a hole D" in diameter to accept the feeder support pipe or rod.

The steel plate shown in Fig. 54 can be made from an electrical junction box cover. Drill the eight holes to the pattern shown, countersink them, and screw the plate firmly to one of the 4"×4" blocks.

Cut out the remaining pieces to the dimensions given. Use a no. 9 drill for the screw holes marked on the 18" ribs. Nail or screw the two 12" and 18" ribs to both 4"×4" blocks and carefully centre the resulting assembly on the inverted tray with the 18" ribs parallel to the 28" edges. With ten no. 10 F.H. or R.H. steel screws 2½" long, with washers under their heads, screw the 18" ribs to the tray. The washers should be thick enough to prevent the screws from breaking through, which would allow moisture to rust the screws.

On the top of the tray, mark out and drill eight countersunk holes (no. 9 drill) directly above the 12" ribs and screw them to the tray with 2" F.H. screws. Set the heads well down and cover them with sealant.

TRAY FEEDERS

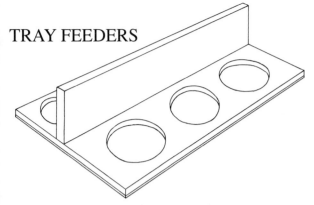

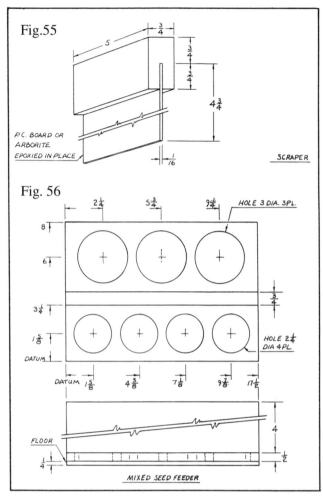

Fig.55

P.C. BOARD OR ARBORITE. EPOXIED IN PLACE

SCRAPER

Fig. 56

HOLE 3 DIA. 3PL.

HOLE 2¼ DIA 4 PL.

DATUM

FLOOR

MIXED SEED FEEDER

The simplest tray feeder is a gardener's wooden seed flat resting on a window sill or other suitable ledge. Photos 15 and 16 show my own tray feeder and how wooden turnbuckles hold it onto a veranda sill in place of one of the screens. A second screen is removed from the other side of the veranda to allow the birds to fly through. Two more trays are located about 18″ off the floor in the veranda itself.

Mixed small seeds are favoured by the small sparrow-type birds and most of these prefer to eat on the ground. Throwing seed on the ground is wasteful and weed promoting, so a shallow tray under a hopper feeder may solve the problem. The illustration above shows a partitioned version which just might allow two birds to feed simultaneously.

CONSTRUCTION

The seed receptacles are simply round holes cut completely through ½″ thick exterior grade plywood to the dimensions of Fig. 56. The floor is a piece of ¼″ plywood which is glued and nailed on after the edges of the holes have been sanded smooth. Half-inch deep holes are amply deep enough as only sufficient seed to cover the floor of each hole should be used. The central plywood partition forms a handle and is best screwed on with three no. 8 F.H. steel screws 1¾″ long. When large numbers of birds are involved, a bigger, open tray about 18″×24″ with 1″ walls is very useful.

A roof on a tray feeder is of marginal help. All four sides should be open, and the overhanging eaves should be at least 10″ above the tray. Such a roof may divert vertically falling rain, but bad weather usually means wind and blowing snow or rain, to which such a roof is no obstacle and the tray and its feed get soaked just the same.

FEEDER LOCATION

The presence of nesting boxes usually tends to increase the number of birds in your general area, the birds being spaced out according to their claimed territories. When a feeding station is established for winter, however, the temporary nesting-season territories no longer pertain. Indeed, most of their former owners are away on migration, and so are not even with us. Even birds which breed locally may migrate and be replaced by birds of the same species from more northerly areas.

The pattern of association therefore has changed to one of local concentration — around the feeder. The pecking order becomes very apparent, for nature rightly demands that only the strongest shall survive, and the strongest eat first.

We may be wrong, but in designing feeders, we often try to ensure that several birds can eat at once, so that the lower ranks get their share. As a dependable food supply attracts additional birds, the resulting concentration tends to attract predators, so feeder placement is very important to the customers.

Birds distrust any kind of enclosure, a solid-sided, roofed windvane type of feeder for example, so an open type of feeder is preferable. But even an open-tray feeder will not be much patronised if it is situated a long way from cover of some kind. Hence, to be successful a feeder must be not more than 10 feet from say, cedar bush, small evergreens or a few densely branched, brushy deciduous trees. Birds are constantly on guard against threats. Even if the danger is seen in time, ten feet probably seems like ten miles to a potential victim.

My own feeder, in its well sheltered fly-through veranda has mixed bush no more than seven feet away and I cannot recall a hawk attack in 18 years. Once started though, such attacks would probably be repeated until either you put a stop to them or there were no birds left. Such dilemmas are the result of the man-made concentrations of birds which occur around a feeder, but the long term results of winter feeding are undoubtedly beneficial, as long as the supply is consistent and free of even short periodic famines.

If the feeder is placed low down and too close to cover, cats can hide in the cover and get close enough to attack; also, squirrels can use it to leap onto the feeder. Just how far a squirrel can jump varies with the available height and the springiness of the take-off branch. As there are always a few Olympic class squirrels about, it is best to add a couple of feet to your initial long jump guesstimate.

Squirrels are worthy opponents and they often figure out ways around the various cones, rollers and drop-down rigs we think up to foil them. Many such devices ice up, others jam, or prove inadequate, but squirrels often teach us a thing or two when we pit our wits against them. Two methods to try are the usual galvanised steel cone of Fig. 57 to stop pole climbers, and two 12″ metal or plastic shields, such as old 78 RPM phonograph discs, to stop the tightrope artists (Fig. 58). It may be necessary to enlarge the holes in the old discs, as they should be pressed onto a few turns of fabric tape such as linen, to prevent localised wear on the clothesline. Both these protective methods are undoubtedly reliable — theoretically!

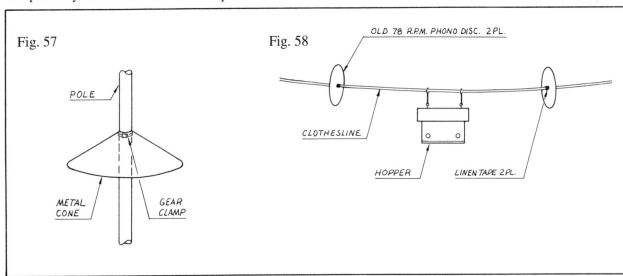

Fig. 57

POLE

METAL CONE

GEAR CLAMP

Fig. 58

OLD 78 R.P.M. PHONO DISC. 2 PL.

CLOTHESLINE

HOPPER

LINEN TAPE 2 PL.

HUMMINGBIRD FEEDERS

When winter birdfeeding declines, then ceases altogether, it is good to be able to cater for summer visitors as intriguing as the hummingbirds.

Small vials, pill containers and tiny bottles about 1½″ long can be wired to hang at 45 degrees from stakes or small poles to make miniature feeding stations. These should preferably be out of sight of each other to avoid potential disputes. They should contain a solution of 1 part sugar to 4 parts of water; some people, however, use two teaspoonfuls of sugar to a cup of water. The wire loop around the neck of each receptacle must have something red included in it; a twist of ribbon, or better still, a plastic flower, provides an excellent attraction. For Hummers, red seems to be no. 1, and yellow, no. 2, but some people find the reverse is true.

Larger feeders, hanging from soffits, crossbars, tree branches and other overhangs also work very well and are available in hardware stores, garden equipment outlets and feed and seed supply houses. As they are almost always made from plastic, these store bought feeders are quite inexpensive. Aside from their feeding ports, most are also totally enclosed and so are much to be preferred over small open mouthed jars, for they are dustproof and easier to maintain and keep clean. Buy a red one, with perhaps a touch of yellow on it.

Ants are to hummingbird feeders as squirrels are to seed feeders, and their ingenuity, persistence and endurance are every bit as remarkable. About the only thing that might stop ants is to coat a section of the feeder's suspension wire with flypaper or a sticky goop such as Tanglefoot paste. I would still back the ants, nevertheless. After a few casualties, they will probably figure out how to bridge the mire or to drop onto the feeder from directly above it. We may not like ants, but we cannot but admire their capabilities.

BIRDFOOD

With most people, a mention of birdfood brings to mind breadcrumbs, and many now ardent birdfeeding addicts started out by offering cake crumbs and the broken up crusts of bread and pies. Although these unduly processed items are more filling than nutritious, they are accepted by most birds. In fact, seed-based food and, more to the point, the seeds themselves, constitute the vast bulk of the food we supply to birds. The remaining items include peanuts and suet and sometimes coconut and crushed walnut kernels.

Grit and water are also required, but most people assume that other sources of both are available, and the birds do seem to find them. Calcium-containing grit is often found along winter roadsides. Birds undoubtedly lose a little of their vital body heat when forced to eat snow to obtain water, but it is best left that way.

Although heated birdbaths are available for winter use, their use in freezing temperatures can prove dangerous should a bird be tempted to take a bath instead of a drink. The bitter winter cold of the northern U.S.A. and Canada can freeze wet feet and feathers solid in a matter of minutes — and the bird quickly dies. It therefore seems best if we do not provide birds with water when all natural sources of it are frozen and inaccessible.

Sunflowers provide what is probably the most popular item on the avian menu, particularly the Blue Jays, chickadees and grosbeaks. As described earlier, a hopper for sunflower seeds with a few peanut hearts thrown in enables a fairer distribution together with less frequent replenishment. When offered in an open tray, sunflower seeds will disappear rapidly. Blue Jays will load up a dozen at a time and stash them away. The seeds will vanish even faster if a flock of grosbeaks appears on the scene. Being relatively powerful, these two species leave almost nothing for the chickadees, who can only airlift the seeds out one or two at a time. A hopper helps to equalize matters.

Birdseed mixes generally include cracked corn, buckwheat, rapeseed, various canary seeds, flax, millet and some quantities of the more expensive sunflower seeds and crushed peanut hearts. Oats, wheat and hemp seed may also be present in mixes, but untreated hemp seed may be hard to find due to its marijuana connection. A small tray feeder will enable you to experiment with various seed mixes to see what goes down best in your area. Some seeds, such as niger, may have to be bought separately.

Where possible, tray feeders should be replenished when empty, which usually means every hour or two during the day. Squirrels, Blue Jays and even grosbeaks retire earlier in the afternoon than smaller birds. Probably due to their size, their body heat build-up allows a longer sleep. This is very convenient for birds like chickadees and American Tree Sparrows whom we should never allow to retire hungry. Feeder replenishment late in the day is therefore even more essential than when the sun is higher.

Seed in trays should only cover the floor lightly, because ground-feeding birds such as juncos will only scatter deep seed layers to find what they want to eat. Each species will only eat certain seeds and foods and will ignore the rest. Snow often covers this uneaten food and it then goes to waste.

'Your' birds are usually not far away when you put food out for them and generally soon appear when they hear your activity, but they quickly learn a personal come-and-get-it signal and respond even faster. Often a door closing is enough to alert them, but more distinctive sounds are easy to make. I flick my fingernails across the tiny spike which projects from under a small plastic yogurt container which gives a loud tock-tock noise.

How closely the birds will approach you depends on your patience and perseverance in demonstrating your genuine affection for them. Chickadees are about the easiest birds to coax to your fingers, but even so, you may not succeed at the first try.

Wear the same clothes for each feeding. If a large blue creature with grey legs offers them food in the morning and a large red one with brown legs does likewise in the afternoon, that makes two large creatures for the birds to cope with. Try not to yawn, smile, show your teeth or swallow, as such motions indicate you are about to eat, and the birds won't wait to find out that you don't have them on your menu.

Often it is too cold to wait for long, so if the birds have not been fed for half an hour or so, they will be keener for food. Keeping still is easier if you are sitting. Your hands, with a few sunflower seeds in them, can then rest on your thighs.

It is much harder to finger-tame the sparrow types who eat the small seed mixes, and under cold conditions, it is hardly worthwhile to offer such seed by hand; it is best left on the tray feeder.

Seeds vary hygroscopically, but cracked corn soaks up water quickly, solidifies, and then turns mouldy. As mouldy food is often poisonous, it is best to remove any accumulation of slush and wet food residues as they occur.

Seeds and husks are inevitable under a raised feeder but there is usually some small creature who benefits from these somewhat untidy leftovers. Seeds are great survivors, however, and a few always make it through the winter to grow into unfamiliar plants next summer.

It is important to keep on feeding until the swallows return in spring as the welcome departure of the snow does not bring any sudden abundance of natural bird food. Snow and sleet storms may return for a few days, insects take a while to appear, and cold wet weather and hunger can still take their toll.

SUET

It is horrifyingly true that almost all our food, and consequently what we feed to birds, is to various degrees poisoned, for we are apparently unable, or unwilling, to grow our food without using injurious chemicals and food additives. Being at the top of the food chain, animals tend to concentrate these chemicals in the fat of their bodies - suet. Because of this I often wonder if we do birds any favour by feeding them suet, government inspected though it may be.

Suet admittedly goes down well with chickadees, nuthatches, woodpeckers and other birds, and it is about all we can offer in place of the insects they prefer but which are not available in winter. As the birds involved do find some other proteins from what few larvae they discover in winter, perhaps such suet as they eat brings them little harm.

Most meat vending food stores will give suet away free, and as a feeder is unnecessary to offer it to the birds, the price is right. Because of the previously mentioned cold metal adhesions, metal mesh or chick wire suet holders are very undesirable and should not be used. All that is needed is an old plastic mesh bag hung on a clothesline or from an overhanging tree branch. A cone type squirrel deflector, like that of Fig. 57, may be required above the suet bag. As suet is a messy, decaying sort of proposition, a temporary throw-away onion bag is much more hygienic than a permanent installation.

It is best to offer suet by itself; there is no need to drill holes in a log and brew up a hot suet-and-seed mixture. Birds wanting suet will ignore the seeds and waste them, and if they want seeds they won't bother with the suet, so separate sources are best.

CAUTION: The cold weather of winter tends to keep suet fairly firm and sanitary but all suet should be removed at the onset of warmer weather in spring. When warmed, suet liquifies somewhat and becomes greasy, and the greasy fluid contaminates bird feathers very readily. The trouble usually starts around the bird's head, which it pokes into holes in the suet. As the bird cannot remove the grease, infection often sets in and death may result. Suet should therefore be examined periodically and when it is found to be liquifying, even slightly, it should be removed immediately.

PEANUT BUTTER

CAUTION: Don't use it. There is some controversy about this well known viscous paste, but there is no doubt in my mind whatever that it has killed many birds. See "Hand Taming Wild Birds at the Feeder" by A. G. Martin, P. 19. Peanut butter is extremely sticky and difficult to remove, and even if it does not choke the bird initially, it seriously disrupts its gravelly digestive system and so can bring death later on. This is hard to demonstrate to those who hold it harmless, because the resulting corpses are not available to convince them. In my opinion any soft cloying food such as peanut butter or creamed cheese, both of which stick to our own throats after swallowing, will probably choke a bird and so has no place on a feeder.

When we have so much safe food to offer birds, it is either careless or callous to give them man-made goop as treacherous as peanut butter, even in the small quantities which most people think of as beneficial. A much safer alternative is crushed peanuts or peanut hearts.

GROWING BIRDSEED

Curiosity once led me to sow an eggcupful of mixed birdseed in a short row, and as might be expected, the result was not exactly a useful coherent crop. It is not always easy to obtain small quantities of the various seeds which make up seed mixes, though they are undoubtedly worth experimenting with. Spray millet, however, as fed to cage birds, is readily obtainable in pet stores and food outlets.

SPRAY MILLET

Millet is enjoyed by most ground feeding birds including Fox, Song, Tree, Vesper and White-throated Sparrows, gold-finches, juncos, Purple Finches, redpolls and siskins. As it is quite expensive, it pays to grow your own and so have plenty of it on hand at all times.

Choose a sunny location in your garden and make 2 or 3 shallow trenches in it about ¾" deep and 2" apart. Select the biggest and ripest head from the package and gently work the seeds off it into the trench as you move along. Avoid heavy concentrations of seed; some of the seeds will not germinate of course, but those that do must have room to grow. Fill in the trench, tamp the soil down level, and water it as necessary.

In southern and eastern Ontario, in Canada, millet takes the whole of the available growing season, in full sun, to mature. Early planting is therefore essential if the crop is to ripen on the stems. An east-west orientation is best for exposing the heads to the sun. As photos 17 and 18 show, spray millet is a grasslike crop about five to six feet tall which will shade adjacent plants from the sun. It is well to allow for this in your annual garden layout. To avoid wind damage, it is best to support the millet and keep it upright. Four T-bar steel posts, one at each end of the row and one each side of it in the middle, hold the requisite lengths of old clothesline or disused electric cable, as seen in photos 17 and 18 on page 62.

As insurance against failure, I actually used seeds from two separate heads to obtain the crop shown, but a single well developed head is ample to plant a row 40' long. The resulting crop should more than fill a bushel basket.

The birds will soon let you know when the crop is ready to eat, but they often prefer it slightly green and before it is fully ripe. Should you run out of sunshine in the fall, the harvested crop can be laid out on sheets of light plywood or sheeting such as Tentest, say 3'×2', and kept out of the rain but in full daylight. The sheets should be exposed to full sun, as available. It is not easy to protect such late ripening millet for long, however, as mice like it too, and you will inevitably lose some heads which they will carry off to eat elsewhere. Lay the sheets on a car hood to hold the mice off. Spray millet is nevertheless very well worth growing, and your parakeet or other cage bird will also be very enthusiastic about it.

SUNFLOWER SEED

Sunflowers are very easy to grow but their dried seeds will never make it to your feeder in winter unless the Blue Jays, chickadees and grosbeaks can be kept at bay while the seeds mature. Blue Jays peck large gaping holes in the backs of the drooping heads of the massive flowers, scattering the seeds on the ground for all and sundry. This may go unnoticed but when you think it's harvest time, you often find that although the goods got to the right address, they got there before you even had chance to mail them.

Should you manage to harvest a few sunflower heads, it is not easy to keep them dry and in the sun until they dry out enough for the seed to be bagged. Mice will again have a stake in the game.

I have not found a good way of protecting sunflower heads for winter feeding but then I have not really tried. Sunflowers bring birds to your garden in both summer and winter and in view of the large quantity of seed needed for winter feeding, you will probably still have to purchase a fair amount of it.

BIRDBATHS

Most birds have an affinity for water and are easily attracted by a garden sprinkler or even the drips from a suspended can with a hole in it. As running water with its bird-attracting sound is not often easy or convenient to arrange, a birdbath is the next best thing in most cases.

The usual store-bought variety is often a shallow concrete bowl on a low pedestal about 10″ to 20″ high, and this is too near the ground for safety. When wet, a bird flies with difficulty and so is vulnerable to predators such as cats and hawks. By raising the bath to at least four feet above ground, we can afford the bathers a better view and make it harder for a cat to surprise them. Hawks pose the same threats at birdbaths as they do at feeders, and similar precautions are necessary. As it is not always feasible to install a fairly heavy concrete birdbath at a height of four feet, it is wise to consider making your own.

BIRDBATH LOCATION

The worst place for a birdbath is on the ground. If such a bath is in the open, there is no protection; if it is near cover, a cat can use it to get close enough to kill. The best place is probably at least four feet up, in a sunny location (after bathing, birds like to stand in the sun for a while to dry out and preen their feathers). It should be six or seven feet from cedar or other dense trees with no undergrowth under them which could hide a cat. The trees must not overhang the bath or provide a place for a cat to lie in wait.

CONSTRUCTION

There are several ready-made objects which, with a little modification, lend themselves to the making of a bird bath.

Cheap plastic pedestal type baths are available, but these are not very durable and may not be worth the trouble of raising them from their usual 24″ to 48″. A pet litter tray might be worth consideration, and a 12″×15″ plastic dish pan can be cut down from its normal 5½″ to 2″. A galvanized steel garbage can lid 18″ in dia. will make an excellent bird bath, as depicted in Fig. 59; its plastic counterpart might also be made to serve.

Whatever method is used, the general idea is to provide an unobstructed shallow trough, not more than 2″ deep, with a flat, tapering slab of rock in it to reduce the water to a depth of about ½″ above the thick part of the slab. The customers can then choose whatever depth suits them.

The garbage can lid of Fig. 59 is quickly made into a birdbath by using its welded-on handle to mount it on a pole similar to that of the hopper feeder of Fig. 54. Drill the two holes in the handle, and then saw through the centre of the handle along the line A - B in Fig. 59. Carefully straighten both pieces of handle, taking care not to lever against the spot welds, and bend each of them with a vise until they lie straight out at 90 degrees from the lid.

As with the feeder, the supporting pole or pipe will be about 1½″ in dia. and some 6½″ feet long, assuming that 2½ feet of it will be in the ground. When easy relocation is required, a solid, heavy based self-supporting pole is very handy, but one for outdoor use may be hard to find. These poles are similar to those used to carry ropes or chains in banks and museums to keep the unwashed from getting their sticky fingers on the goods. As neither establishment is likely to endorse your liberating one of their poles, it is better to try a scrap metal merchant or the local dump.

When a suitable pole has been obtained, cut a 7″×3″ block from say, pine or fir, and make its third dimension a firm fit between the two sections of straightened handle. Drill a close fitting blind hole in the block for your chosen pipe or pole, as shown in Fig. 59, leaving about ⅜″ of wood at the top for support. Fasten the block in place with two no. 8×1″ R.H. steel screws.

Leaves and other debris which may accumulate in the lid are easily removed after working the block upwards off the pole. Inherent inaccuracies usually allow the lid to be rotated to level the rim with the water. As birds have no reason to visit the metal lid unless it contains water, cold weather adhesions are not a problem.

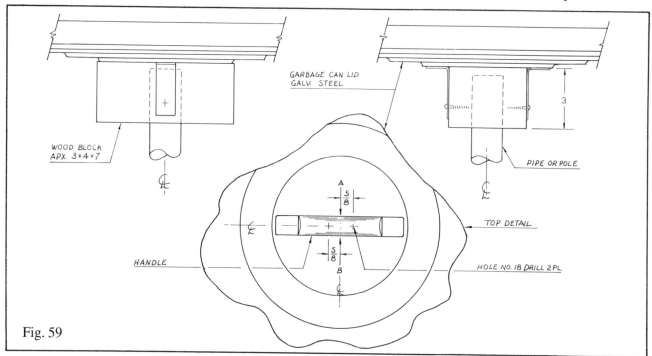

Fig. 59

CHAPTER 7.
BIRD ROOSTING BOXES

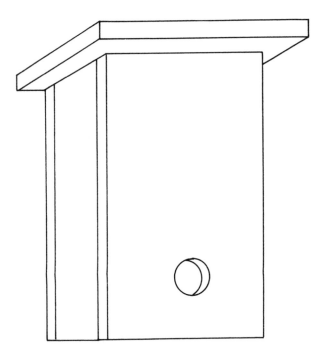

Native birds have long since acclimatized themselves to sleeping outside in winter. It is as well, however, to make some provision for them when there is the possibility of severe conditions, such as a food-restricting ice storm, or extreme cold accompanied by wind. In such conditions the first concern of birds, and other creatures too, is to get out of the wind. Should conditions warrant it, they will indeed gather in a small space and huddle together to conserve their collective body heat. Like ourselves, however, they seem to surrender their personal living space somewhat reluctantly. People, for example, temporarily give up this 'breathing space' in, say, an elevator, and quickly spread out again as soon as they are able. As such bitter cold is not very frequent in winter, it makes sense to create a roosting box which will convert into a nesting box. By this means, a single box will serve both purposes on a year-round basis; it is then no loss if it goes unused as a roosting box in winter.

Providing a roosting box is not, as some people think, simply a matter of leaving a nesting box out all year, because nesting and roosting involve conflicting requirements. Birds just might use a nest box to roost in, if the night is cold enough and there is nothing better available, but a nest box can hardly help them much.

Being generally near the top, the entrance and ventilation holes of a nesting box allow the small amount of rising warmth to escape almost immediately. Simply inverting the front will not work to solve the problem because the birds must remain on the floor, in the arctic-cold air from the entrance hole.

If, however, we invert the front, seal the box, and provide perches in its upper two thirds, then body heat can no longer escape upwards and the birds can sleep above the bitingly cold air on the floor below. In view of their proven winter hardiness, this is as good an arrangement as we need offer them.

Of the wintertime resident birds, only the smallest seem to show any interest whatever in roosting boxes; the larger species such as grosbeaks and Blue Jays evidently have superior thermal characteristics and so need no additional shelter. The combination nesting-roosting box of Fig. 60 is therefore made with chickadees in mind. The box is most likely to be used when the temperature is down to say –40 degrees C. or so, when even a moderate wind can send a cutting slice of cold through the slightest crack. Where such low temperatures are encountered, it seems best to install weatherstripping around three sides of the front, as shown by the shaded areas of Fig. 60.

CONSTRUCTION

Except for a few necessary additions, the combination box of Fig.60 is quite similar in construction to those of Figs. 2 to 6. It is essentially a carefully made bluebird/Tree Swallow size of box with a chickadee-sized entrance hole.

Cut out the pieces accurately from ¾″ thick pine and saw-cut the ladder slots in the front and back (see Fig. 8 detail). The requisite short central ladder slots can be cut by lowering the wood onto the saw blade. If you run the slots fully across the wood, however, drafts must be prevented by filling in both ends of each slot for a distance of 1″ with a mixture of glue and wood filler.
ENTRANCE HOLE: If House Sparrows are a problem, cut out a 1⅛″ dia. hole, otherwise use 1¼″, as chickadees find it easier to use. The front is held on by four catches of the type shown in Fig. 18 and they use the eight catch nails as positioned in Fig. 60. If the catches are to hold firmly in both positions of the front, symmetry is essential, and the nails in the front must lie exactly on the centre lines of its edges. These positions should be carefully marked out.

Mark out and drill the six ½″ dia. holes for the three 6½″ long dowels. It is easiest to align the two sides with each other, clamp them together and drill them as a pair in the drill press. This method will give good hole alignment.

Make the 5″ block which abuts the top of the front and cut the weatherstripping grooves in it and in the front edges of the sides.

The hanger can be purchased or made from a piece of scrap brass or an electrical junction box cover. It is about 2½″×1″×1/16″ with a keyhole cut in it by merging two holes of 7/16″ and 3/16″ dia. The hanger is recessed and held on as shown by two screws.

The box is assembled by nailing the sides to the back, followed by the floor and top, maintaining their alignment meanwhile. See that the 5″ block fits well and aligns with the front edges of the sides. Make and fit the two 5″ strips to the door so that it fits correctly in its two positions.

Make two L.H. and two R.H. hook catches as shown in Fig. 18 and fit them to the front and sides as shown by the nails in Fig. 60. Hammer the nails into the edges of the front as previously marked out, fit the front on the box and draw a line on the side level with the front nail. Fit each catch in turn and locate its pivot nail where it lies on the line.

Cut the 5/32″×3/8″ weatherstripping to suit and fit it in place. Make and fit the two 2½″ wooden turnbuckles. File off the points of any nails or screws which may be projecting inside the box.

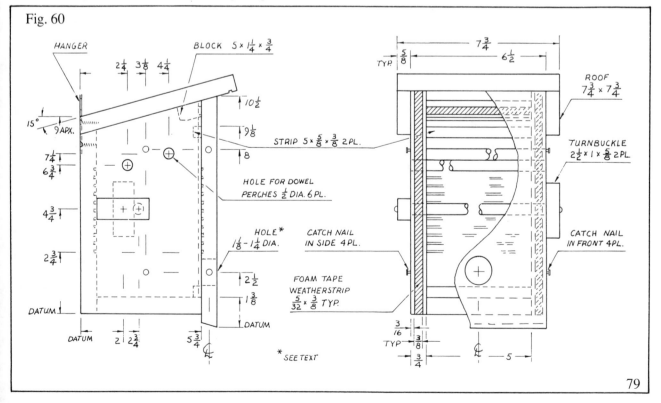

Fig. 60

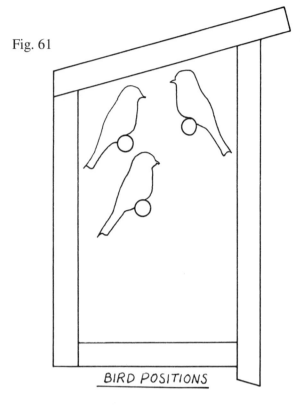

Fig. 61

BIRD POSITIONS

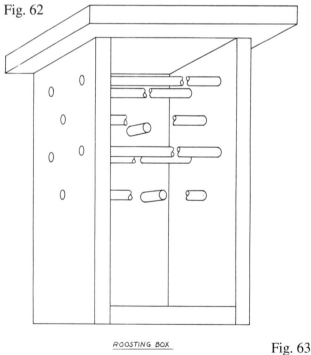

Fig. 62

ROOSTING BOX

In its roosting box mode, the box is assembled as shown in Fig. 60, when it would be capable of housing some 12 birds, say four on each perch. When a nesting box is required, the perches are knocked out with a piece of ⅜″ dowel or a punch, the front is inverted, and the two turnbuckles rotated to cover the lower ½″ holes. If left open, these two holes are low enough to admit drafts which could affect the nestlings; the upper four holes are high enough to provide desirable ventilation.

The placement of the perches allows the birds to take up the assumed positions of Fig. 61, but the birds will have their own ideas about that. It is well to stagger the perches vertically so that the lower ranks stand a sporting chance of avoiding what descends from above during the night. This idea has also been applied to some extent in the taller design of Fig. 62, of which Fig. 63 represents a top view.

No dimensions are given in Fig. 62 as it is intended as a general idea only. The floor area should be very little larger than that of Fig. 61, however, as there is no point in making a large volume box for small birds because their heat would simply dissipate faster. If, after making the versatile box of Fig. 60, droppings indicate its usefulness as a roosting box, something along the lines of Fig. 62 could then be built and tried out as well.

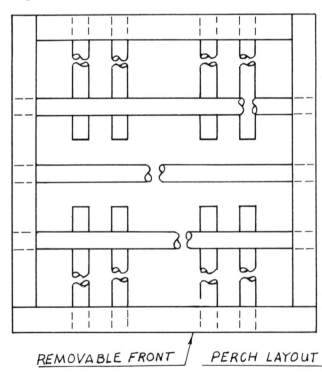

Fig. 63

REMOVABLE FRONT / PERCH LAYOUT

NEST BOX AND
ROOSTING BOX SITES

Chickadees prefer to nest some five to seven feet up in a partially concealed location in mixed bush in which cedar and pine predominate. As they will have some affinity for their nest box, it is as well to set up potential roosting quarters in the same place or nearby, provided it is sufficiently sheltered from the worst of the winter winds.

CHAPTER 8.
BAT HOUSES

Bird nesting boxes are a familiar sight in both city suburbs and countryside of North America, but bat 'nesting boxes' are extremely rare, and in fact, almost unheard of. This is a very regrettable situation, because most bats eat vast numbers of insects during the night just as birds do in daylight and bats are no less important to us than birds.

Bats have long had a totally unjustified bad press. If any creature on this planet needs a public relations boost, it is the bat. It seems there are more than 850 species of bat in the world, and only three of them — in

South America — are Dracula types who drink blood. And none of the others are at all interested in tangling with woman's crowning glory, though they may, very rarely, pass close by to catch a flying insect. Some 18 to 20 species choose to live in Canada.

A few tropical species eat fruit which we would rather eat ourselves, but the vast majority of bats are extremely beneficial in consuming legions of insects that would otherwise make our lives impossible. For us to harass and destroy such valuable allies is most unwise and we shall surely pay dearly if we do not protect them.

As for rabies, you are probably more likely to get it from man's best friend, the family dog, than you are from a bat. Like other animals, bats have their own brands of parasites, internal and external, and their dried droppings can be just as harmful to us as those of birds but none of these factors should single them out for hate and destruction.

There are signs that North Americans are reviewing the bat's public image but we are about 50 years behind the United Kingdom, where there are many informal 'bat clubs'; thousands of bat houses have been set up over the years on both public and private property. The same enlightened approach has spread to Australia, and it is long overdue in Canada and the USA.

After the immense longlasting damage that DDT has caused to wildlife in the world, it is hard to believe that the Province of Ontario still allowed pest control companies to use DDT on bats as late as 1988.

The more enlightened of the pest control companies catch the bats in nets or by hand and release them many miles away. Others may expel the bats with a chemical repellant, or await their usual exit at sundown. In any case, the entry openings are sealed as soon as all the bats are out. This prevents their possible return. A bat house erected nearby would probably stand a good change of occupancy. If you must expel bats, always do so humanely; do not poison or kill them and never should you employ a firm that uses poisons of any kind.

Bats are very unlikely to crash into anybody. Their wonderful radar systems are sensitive enough to enable them to detect and catch tiny insects, on the wing, and in the dark. Avoiding massive creatures like ourselves is child's play to them. On occasion, a bat may prove this by flying round a darkened bedroom, perhaps in a summer cottage, without touching anything, including yourself. A tiny breeze on your face might be the only indication of its presence. All that need be done is to switch the light on, locate the bat, GENTLY enfold it in a thick towel and release it outdoors.

Bats do sometimes occupy attics and may have to be removed. Lighting up the attic with incandescent lamps for 24 hours a day for the roosting season will usually cause them to move out. The often surprisingly small entry points can then be sealed up.

Because bat populations are hard to assess and bats are not easy to study, there is much less information about them than there is on birds. There is little doubt that our bats are in trouble, and the likely causes of their decline are the chemically poisoned insects they eat, and man's increasing disturbance of their underground hibernating quarters. These serious problems can be solved by public enlightenment combined with rapid and sane government action before it is too late.

To pass the winter, some bats migrate, others seek out caves and old mines where the temperature does not drop below freezing. Any bat houses we may erect are therefore only used in spring and summer for the purposes of raising their usual single offspring, and daytime sleeping.

As bats can navigate well and remember locations, they are likely to return each spring to a bat house they discovered and used previously. When kept in good repair, large bat houses might well shelter enough bats each year to form the nocturnal equivalent of a Purple Martin colony.

Bird boxes have been around long enough for their dimensions to have become more or less standardised and well known. Being relatively late arrivals on the human interest scene, bat houses offer more scope for experiment and their potential has yet to be realised. Their designs and measurements are not necessarily carved in granite. Exactly which and what slot widths to offer in them may vary from one area to another, in order to accommodate the species available. Typical slot widths have been incorporated in the following design. Its size is fairly small and larger versions are feasible should the colony grow.

CONSTRUCTION

The bat house shown in Figs. 64 to 66 is best made of rough untreated woods. Rough surfaces are easier for the bats to climb and as bats are susceptible to chemical pollution, all stains, paints and pressure treated woods are to be avoided. Ideally, redwood is about the best choice for the top, front, back and sides (the shell), but cedar or pine may also be used. If pieces of lumber 11" wide are not available, two narrower pieces may be glued together edge-to-edge. The shell of the box can also be made up of several short narrow sections joined edge-to-edge, but with their grain horizontal. This would not be quite as strong, however, because all nailing (except at the top) would be into end grain.

The three partitions can be made from ½" spruce or fir sheeting grade exterior plywood. This plywood is used for roofs and is rough both sides. Usually, bat house partitions are rectangular, as is no. 1. I feel, however, that cutting the lower edges of nos. 2 and 3 into opposing slopes, as shown in Fig. 65, might possibly improve the bats' access. It simulates a greater separation between all three partitions, and so makes them easier to distinguish. Such small changes are often worth a trial.

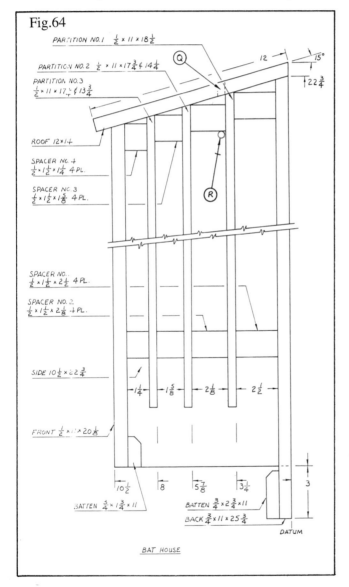

Fig.64

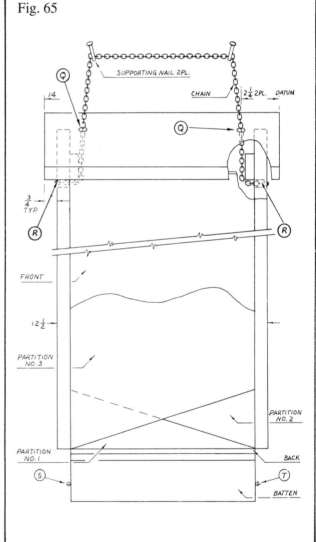

Fig. 65

84

The house is not much more complicated to build than a bird box. Cut out the various pieces to the dimensions given in Figs. 64 and 65. The appearance of the finished house will be improved if the outer surfaces of the roof, front and sides are planed smooth and sanded. Only the edges of the partitions should be sanded, to take care of stray splinters. As the bats' tiny claws grip best in horizontal cracks and cuts, the partitions are best made with their visible grain horizontal. Those areas of the partitions and the inside surfaces of the shell which are not rough enough, should receive additional horizontal scoring. A good method is to draw a large sharp wood rasp, or the end of a body file, sideways across the wood. Holding the free end of the body file still, and rotating the handle end, produces a series of clean cut arcs which also work well. Narrow, well defined cuts are the objective, and they should be nowhere near deep enough to expose the glue.

Nail or screw the battens onto the front and back, and then nail the sides onto the back with 2″ spiral steel nails. With the assembly on its back, temporarily fit the 16 spacers and three partitions in between the sides, and trim the spaces so that the front can lie level with the edges of the sides, from top to bottom. When correctly positioned, glue and nail the ½″ thick spacers to the sides.

Nail the sides through into the front and accurately pencil in the centrelines of the partitions on the sides. On these centrelines, about 4″ apart, mark out and drill holes for 1½″ ring nails. Ensure that each partition in turn is level with the top and aligned centrally with the holes, and nail them in place. As the partitions are only ½″ thick, this requires care. See that no splitting or splintering has occurred and remove any offending nails or splinters.

Try the roof on and plane the tops of the partitions and shell, as required, to obtain a flush fit all round. Nail the top down to the shell with 2½″ spiral steel nails so that ¾″ overhangs both sides equally. Note that the nails penetrating the front and back have to be driven vertically and are not normal to the plane of the roof.

There are several ways of mounting the completed bat house on a tree or building. As with nest boxes of a similar size, plumber's strapping can be bolted to the house sides and nailed to a tree. The back can be made as in Fig. 7, or a chain can be used, as in Fig. 65.

As the box weighs about 20 lb., a substantial steel chain is required, say of the type used to hang fluorescent lights.

The chain is fed through a hole of appropriate size in the roof and fished out through a similarly sized hole in the side. This can be done with a bent piece of wire or a bicycle spoke. A bent nail, its point driven into the side, is used to secure the ends of the chain, as shown in Fig. 66.

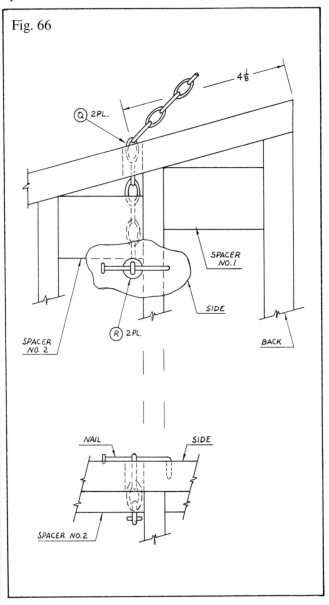

Fig. 66

HOUSE SITE

Bats prefer to roost in the general vicinity of water, not much more than a quarter of a mile from a river, creek, pond or swamp. The house should be fastened to a tree or building, not less than ten feet above ground, and facing away from the worst-weather wind. As bats apparently enjoy heat and humidity, a southerly aspect for bat houses seems best for most of the North American continent.

At the chosen site, drive two 4″ nails into the tree or supporting structure (see Fig. 65), and hang the house up. Make sure the chain is not kinked or twisted, and if possible, slip two small nails through the links at point Q in Fig. 66. These will prevent the chain from slipping when slack. Force a good waterproof sealant into both Q and R holes (Fig. 66), plugging all four holes thoroughly. See that the sealant mounds up somewhat, so that no hollows are present. Water can then run off satisfactorily. Steady the house against shifting by driving in two 3½″ nails, flush with the batten, at points S and T in Fig. 65.

Bats don't take kindly to disturbances. If, in due course, they indicate their presence with a few droppings, there may be no further offerings if you shine your inspection flashlight upwards too frequently.

GLOSSARY

Batten wooden strip, generally for strengthening
Bevel see 'chamfer'
BH back height
Chamfer a bevel, a cut across a corner, or along an edge
CL clearance
℄ centre line
Cors. corners
C.R. cold rolled i.e. C.R.S. - cold rolled steel
C'sunk countersunk
Datum basic line from which measurements are taken
Dia. diameter
DP deep
FH front height
FH screw flat-headed screws (for countersunk holes)

Galv. galvanized
GB glue block
HD hole diameter
HH hole height
LG long
LH left hand (ed)
No. number
Nom. nominal
Pl. the item indicated occurs in other places in the figure
Rad. radius
RH right hand (ed)
R.H. screws round-headed screws
RPM revolutions per minute
Thk. thick
Typ. typical, occurs elsewhere in the figure

INDEX